Fancy Ice Carving

August Forster

Author of *American Culinary Art*
How to Make Your Own Hors d'Oeuvres

COACHWHIP PUBLICATIONS
GREENVILLE, OHIO

Fancy Ice-Carving, by August Forster
First published 1947.
© 2013 Coachwhip Publications
No claims made on public domain material.
Front cover: Carved ice cake stand (CC) Tracy Hunter

ISBN 1-61646-176-4
ISBN-13 978-1-61646-176-8

CoachwhipBooks.com

PUBLISHER'S NOTE

The calls for this book have been so great in the few months it has been out of print that we are happy to have the opportunity of reproducing it for our customers.

There can be no doubt of Mr. Forster's outstanding ability as a food decorator. He has received many awards for his work in Gum Sugar, Wax, Papier-Maché, Vegetable Carving, and Fruit Hors d'Oeuvres. He has also received a Special Award from the American Sugar Refining Company.

August Forster was born in Zurich, Switzerland and received his training in many of Europe's finest hotels. He started the first professional cooking school for the Chicago Board of Education and is now engaged in teaching and writing for adults and High School students.

CONTENTS

CONTENTS

PREFACE

This book is so written that it enables every man to learn the art of ice carving without previous knowledge or the help of instruction from others.

My eighteen years of instructing the culinary art chefs, war veterans, and youngsters for the Chicago Board of Education have convinced me that I can teach this art to anyone if they will follow the rules. But these rules must be followed, line for line. This simplified way of learning will capture your interest to such an extent that you will want to do even more than I would normally expect, particularly if luck is with you and you do not break too many pieces in the beginning.

At the end of the thirty lessons in this book, you will find you are able to draw or select your own ice design and carve any that you wish. Ice pieces are made with a chisel or with forms and molds and belong to the art of sculpture. Remember that practice makes perfect.

This skillful art is not only fascinating; financially it is of direct benefit to you and to your employer. It means many extra dollars for both.

I leave the book in your hands knowing it has been the means of making you an Ice Artist.

AUGUST FORSTER

Chapter One

DIFFERENT KINDS
OF ICE AND ICE CARVINGS

Every successful restaurant and hotel manager wants a chef or cook who knows how to make ice carvings. It means additional revenue and adds to the prestige of the establishment. It enhances the beauty of buffet tables, banquets, and parties of all kinds.

The large pieces may be used as center pieces; the smaller ones for punch bowls, appetizers, salads, sandwiches, canapes, fish, cold meats, desserts, and ice creams.

The effectiveness of ice carvings is increased by the insertion of a small electric battery and light bulb. When illuminated, their beauty is increased, particularly for an evening affair.

Natural Ice. This is harvested from lakes and rivers during the winter and stored in barns, covered with straw or sawdust to hold over the summer. It is as satisfactory to carve as artificial ice if care is taken that it is not cracked as a result of rough handling. It has the advantage of being cut in larger cakes from which nicer pieces may be carved.

Never use dirty ice and never work in sunlight as the ice melts too fast. When a piece is completed it should be placed in a cooler with temperature below freezing. Never use milky ice except when the pieces are to be photographed. It is best for this purpose as clear ice does not photograph well.

Artificial Ice. This is used in cities the year around for ice carving. It has advantages and disadvantages. It is of uniform size and may be ordered accordingly. The freezing is perfect and the ice has a fine glare. However, when it is carved in a warm room it soon becomes brittle and often breaks just about the time the piece is finished. Beginners should not become discouraged when this happens as they soon learn to carve with more delicate strokes. When the ice is shiny throughout the entire piece be on guard against breakage.

Many people carve the ice in the cooler in which case it never melts.

Finished ice pieces should be washed off with cold water to free them from shavings, then placed in the cooler at a temperature below freezing. When large pieces are to be made the blocks must be frozen together. In this case each block is watered and placed one on top of the other and frozen over night at five degrees below zero.

Fresh flowers, flags, birds, and often fish may be frozen in the ice. In such cases, little carving is required unless an additional piece of ice is used as a standard.

Ice pieces should be made the day before they are to be used as they look much better the second day.

Colored Ice. Another advantage of artificial ice is that the water may be colored before it is frozen and colored ice carvings are very attractive. Fruit coloring is used and it should be well mixed when placed in the water so that it will not remain on the bottom. This water requires a great deal of color. Test the amount of coloring by putting some of the water in a glass. Look through it and see if the coloring is sufficient. After freezing, the ice is carved the same as for any other piece.

If you do not freeze your own ice, you can furnish the factory with the coloring and have any color you wish. Colored ice carvings are particularly attractive when illuminated.

Decorating with Colored Water. This can be done only with carved pieces that may be laid flat. In the parts of the piece you wish decorated, carve a groove one or two inches thick. When the grooving is in danger of breaking the piece, use hot rods of iron to burn the groove into the ice. Extreme care must be used in controlling the hot water which results from this burning. A wet towel held in one hand may be used to wipe up this water.

Be sure the ice carving is on a level surface and that the groove is filled to the top with colored water. The filling should be done in the cooler where the piece should remain over night. The next morning it might be necessary to go over the grooves with a chisel to round or even them off.

Another method of decoration is to spray colored water on the ice. The cooler must be 10 degrees below zero when the colors are sprayed on the ice. The amount of water sprayed on (the thickness) depends upon how long it will remain in the dining room. A thickness of one inch when taken directly out of the cooler will keep at least 30 minutes in the dining room without changing color.

A common fly spray may be used for this but the water must be cold and care must be taken that the colors do not run together. Chocolate powder, flour, silver or gold dust may also be used for spraying. There is no end to the powders that may be sprayed on ice when they are used only for show pieces and do not come in contact with food. Do not use too much color on your ice piece so as to make it garish and in bad taste. And do not try to spray with color unless you can work in a cooler 10 degrees below zero.

Carving by Steam or Electricity. In recent years ice has been carved successfully by the use of steam. Most restaurants and hotels have steam available and it may be piped directly to the cooler where the ice carving is done. A rubber hose may be attached to the pipe line. Have this several feet long for the sake of flexibility. At the end of this hose, attach a metal nozzle one-half foot long with an opening at one end one-eighth inch in diameter. The nozzle should be thin, flat instead of round, with a handle of any convenient size so it will not be clumsy to hold in the hand.

The steam cuts like a knife and does the work faster so that you do not get as wet as when shaving the ice. Have a pitcher of cold water on hand and a wet towel to control the hot water running off. This can do damage eating into the carved piece where you do not intend it to.

Carving with an electric rod is much the same as with steam but it is dangerous and I do not recommend it.

Chapter Two

LESSONS

There are a few rules you must keep in mind before we start on the lessons.

1. Remember that the material you are working with is slippery. It can slide easily from a table or out of your hands. It is wise to place one or two towels under the ice. This makes it more maneuverable for you in case you must turn it.

2. Remember that you are working with fragile material which breaks easily if you apply too much strength on your chisel. Ice pieces soon become softer and, therefore, more brittle requiring more care and caution and less hitting strength with the chisel. Blocks must be laid down carefully to avoid breaking. This usually occurs at the finish point.

3. Never start to work on ice before it is trimmed correctly. Failure to do this means waste of time and money.

4. Follow the lessons in order as they are given to you. After you have finished the first five or six pieces you may want to skip over a few and make the more difficult ones. Don't do it. Each lesson is worked out according to your progress. Though they may look simple, they are hard to make. Each design is necessary before you pass on to the next.

When you have completed the thirty lessons in this book you should be able to do almost any piece of carving for which you have a request. You will get orders for holiday parties, weddings, birthday parties, and banquets. Especially will you be asked to do pieces for buffet tables. You might get an order for something you have never made but you will be able to do it because of your past experience. After these thirty lessons you may try any of the designs in the book or make your own drawings and follow them.

We are now ready for the first lesson.

11

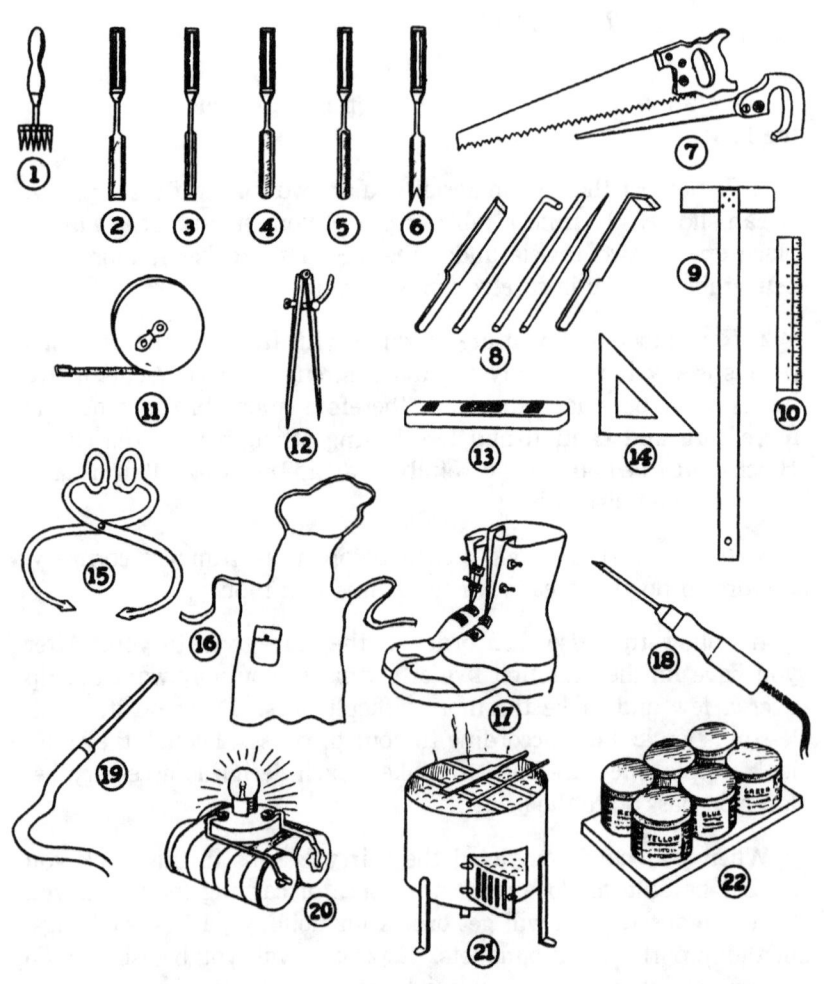

TOOLS REQUIRED FOR ICE CARVING

1. Ice Shaver
2. Chisel - 2″ wide
3. Chisel - 1″ wide
4. Chisel, half round - 1″
5. Chisel, round - 1″
6. Chisel, V-shaped - ¼″ deep
7. Saws - 1 large, 1 small
8. Irons, flat, right angle, and straight - 15″ long
9. T-square
10. Ruler
11. Tape measure
12. Geometrical compass
13. Water level
14. Right angle
15. Ice tongs
16. Leather apron
17. Rubber shoes
18. Insulated electric rod
19. Steam pipe
20. Electric battery with bulb
21. Heating apparatus for irons
22. Fruit coloring

BEGINNER'S TOOLS

Two sharp chisels, a ruler, an ice shaver, one saw, and one hot iron will serve your purpose for a long time. Many ice carvers never use more than these.

LESSON 1

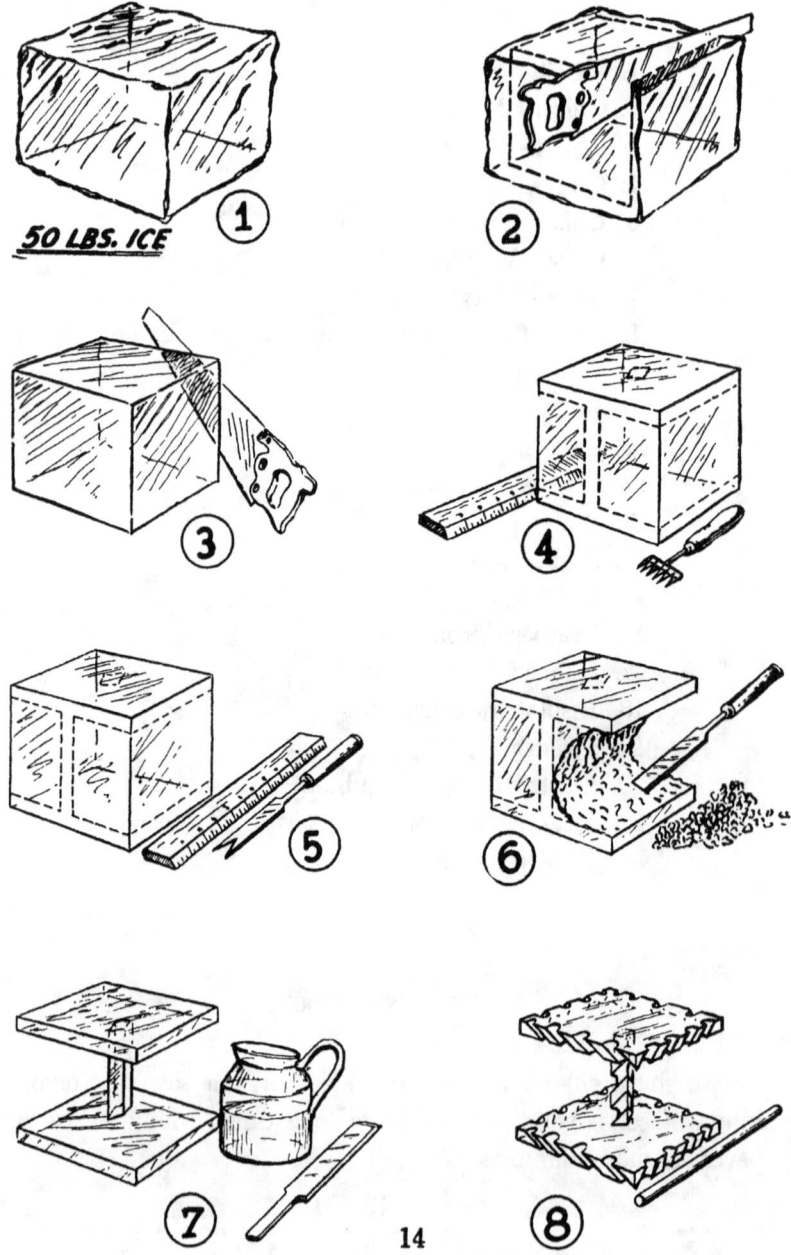

50 LBS. ICE

① ② ③ ④ ⑤ ⑥ ⑦ ⑧

14

APPETIZER STAND

1. Ice, as it comes from the ice house in 50-pound cakes, is rough and uneven.

2. With the aid of a ruler and an ice shaver, mark your ice in a perfect square. Next, saw it square on all four sides. Do not start to carve until the block of ice is perfectly square.

3. The perfect piece of ice is now ready to be marked.

4. With the aid of a ruler and the ice shaver, mark the border one inch wide at top and bottom and mark the post in the middle.

5. The marked ice is now followed with a V-chisel to make a deeper impression. Use the ruler to be sure the lines are straight.

6. With a 2-inch chisel, carve the ice out from all sides, leaving a post in the center. When all the ice is removed, chisel the post square in shape, not touching the top or bottom levels of the stand.

7. With the aid of a hot iron, burn the corners square and wash the ice off with cold water.

8. When the piece is finished, burn lines into the ice ½-inch deep with a round hot iron.

LESSON 2

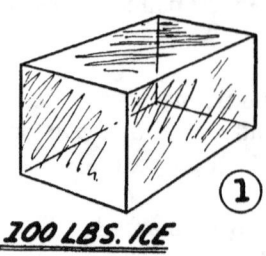

100 LBS. ICE

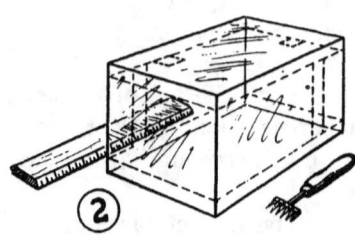

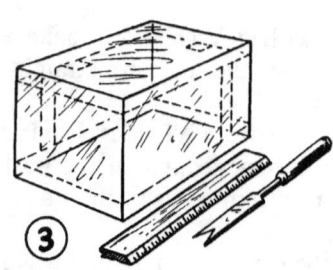

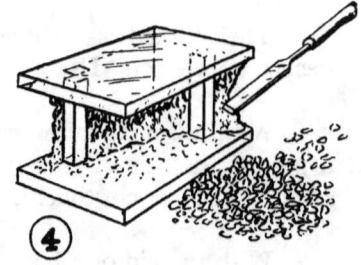

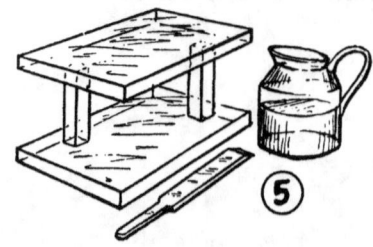

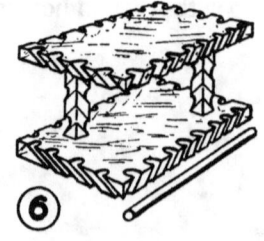

DOUBLE APPETIZER STAND

1. The ice is squared and sawed ready to be marked.

2. Mark the top and bottom border one inch wide on all four sides of the block. With a ruler and ice shaver mark also the two posts on the left and right side of the block.

3. Carve these lines again with the V-chisel and with the aid of a ruler, assuring straight lines.

4. With the two-inch chisel, starting in the front of the block, carve out the ice not quite to the center. Turn the ice around and repeat the same operation, always allowing for the posts. When this is accomplished, carve out the posts.

5. Wash the ice off and burn the posts square with a hot iron.

6. With a long round iron, burn the lines into the ice one-half inch thick. Food may be served on the top of this stand as well as on the bottom.

LESSON 3

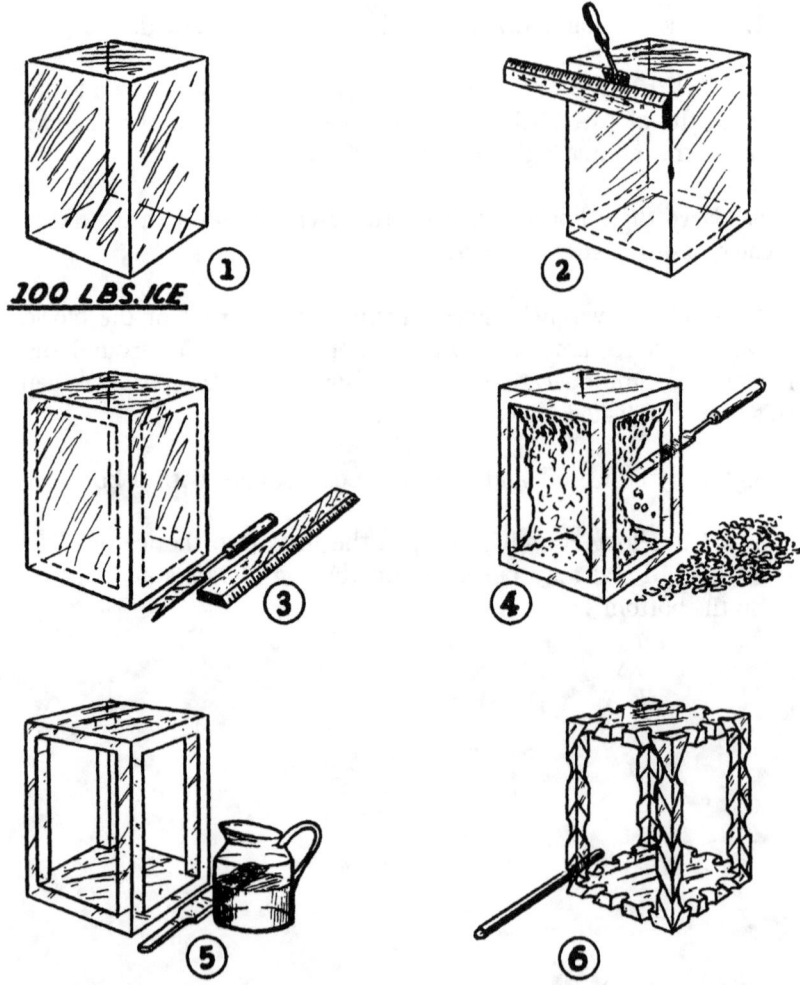

200 LBS. ICE

① ② ③ ④ ⑤ ⑥

SANDWICH STAND

1. Squared ice ready to be marked.

2. With the aid of a ruler and ice shaver, mark a one-inch border, top and bottom and on all four sides for the posts.

3. Carve these lines again with the aid of the V-chisel and a ruler, making them deeper.

4. Remove the ice with a two-inch chisel but do not touch the posts.

5. Burn the posts square with a hot, flat iron and wash the ice off with cold water.

6. With a round, hot iron, burn the lines in one-half inch deep. Food may be served on the top and bottom of this stand.

LESSON 4

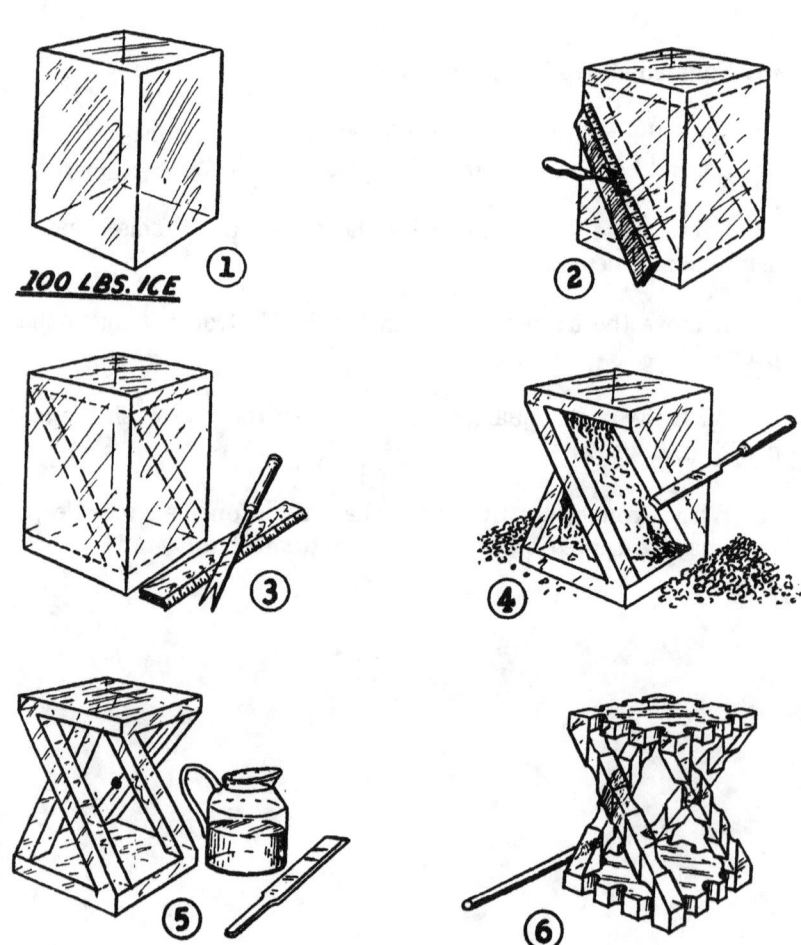

100 LBS. ICE ①

②

③

④

⑤

⑥

DECORATIVE SANDWICH STAND

1. Ice trimmed, ready to be carved.

2. Mark the ice as indicated with the aid of a ruler and ice shaver.

3. Deepen the lines with the V-chisel and the ruler. Keep them perfectly straight.

4. Carve the sides out with the two-inch chisel. As you get deeper into the piece, use the one-inch chisel. From this point, do not put heavy pressure on the chisel.

5. Burn the posts, making sharp edges. Pour cold water over the piece.

6. With a round hot iron, burn lines into the piece one-half inch thick.

LESSON 5

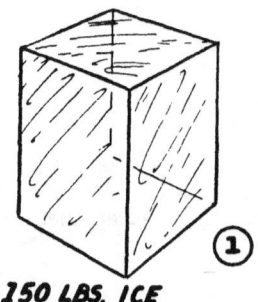

150 LBS. ICE

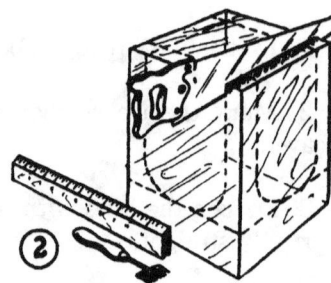

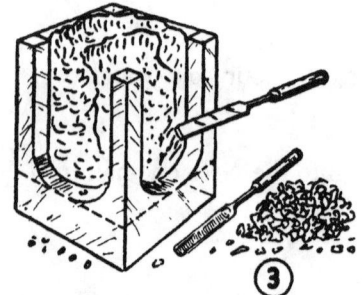

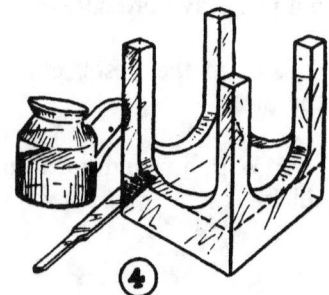

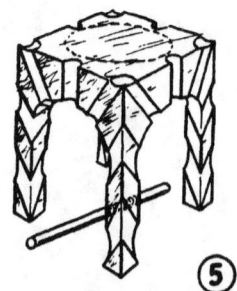

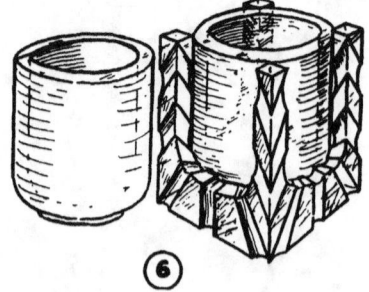

22

COMBINATION SANDWICH
AND SALAD STAND

1. Ice trimmed, ready to be carved. Must be perfectly square.

2. The dotted lines show the markings to be made with the ruler and shaver one inch in from each of the four sides on top. The lines at the bottom show how far down to saw.

3. Remove the inside ice with a two-inch chisel and use a round chisel to round off the bottom.

4. Wash off the piece with cold water and place a bowl of hot water between the posts. In that way, the bowl will carve out its own place to fit it exactly. When the bowl has reached its proper depth in the ice, remove it. When ready for service, fill the bowl with salad or caviar.

5. Burn lines into the ice with a straight iron.

6. The stand may be used upright with the bowl at the side or it may be used with the bowl placed in the center, filled with salad.

LESSON 6

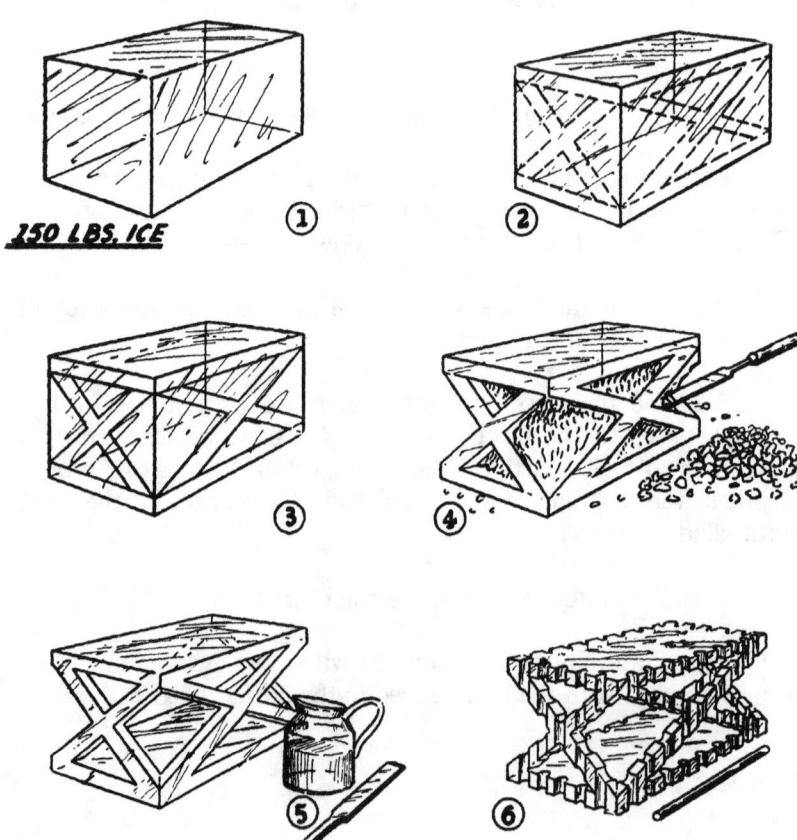

150 LBS. ICE

①

②

③

④

⑤

⑥

24

HORS d'OEUVRE STAND

1. Ice trimmed and ready for use.

2. Ice marked with ruler and ice shaver.

3. Lines deepened with V-chisel.

4. Ice carved out between the posts. Start on one corner first and chisel half way into the ice block.

5. Burn the post with a flat iron to sharpen the edges. Wash with cold water.

6. Burn the lines in with a round iron. Handle the piece with care and keep it in a cold ice box until needed.

LESSON 7

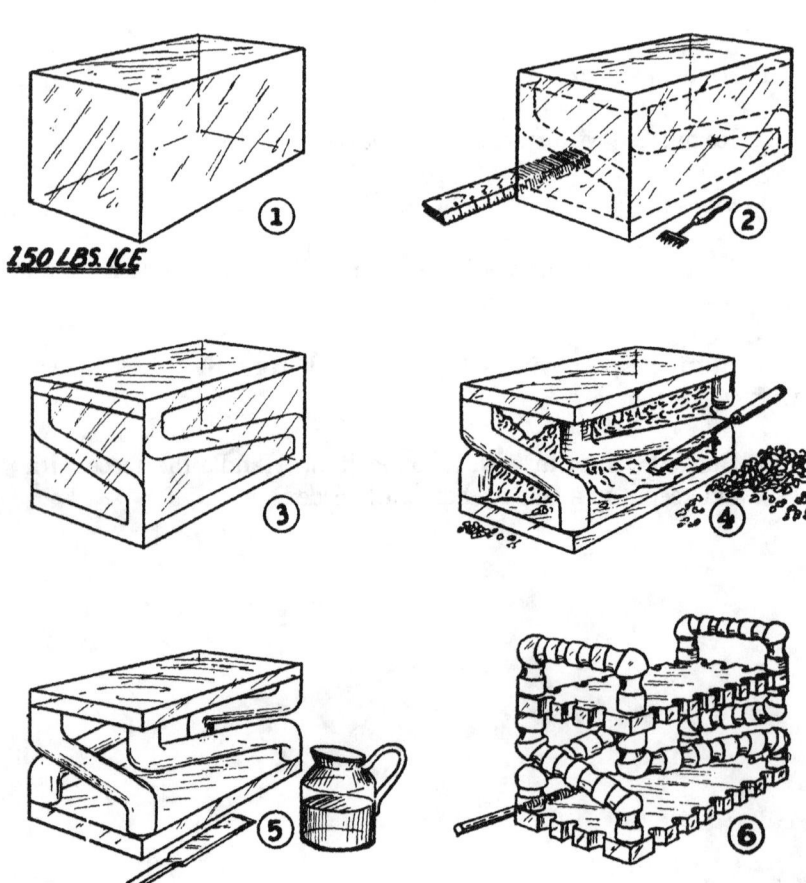

250 LBS. ICE

ASSORTED RELISH STAND

1. Ice trimmed and ready for use.

2. Mark in design as shown.

3. Deepen impressions with V-chisel.

4. Carve out the ice, starting from the corner. Make the posts two inches thick and carve out all the ice around them.

5. Remove all unnecessary ice with the aid of a half round chisel, making round posts. Burn in the lines with a round iron. If the two handles are desired, this will require 200 pounds of ice.

This piece may be used for serving hors d'oeuvres, relishes, cold meats, fish, poultry, or ice cream. It is a delicate piece and extreme care must be taken in the carving.

LESSON 8

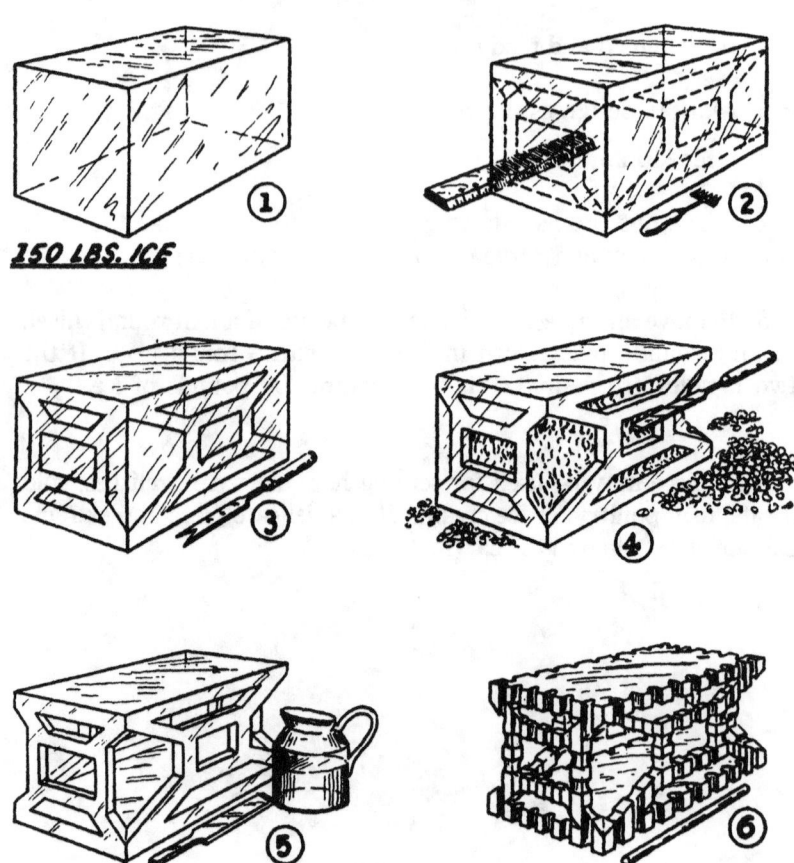

150 LBS. ICE

ASSORTED CANAPE STAND

1. Ice trimmed and ready for use.

2. Ice correctly marked.

3. Lines deepened with V-chisel.

4. Carve the ice out around the design, starting at the corner.

5. Burn the edges so they are sharp and straight and wash the piece off with cold water. Use a flat iron to burn the edges.

6. Burn the heavy lines with a round iron and the small lines with a hot wire. This is an all-purpose piece, the same as the one in the previous lesson. Extreme care is required in the finishing.

LESSON 9

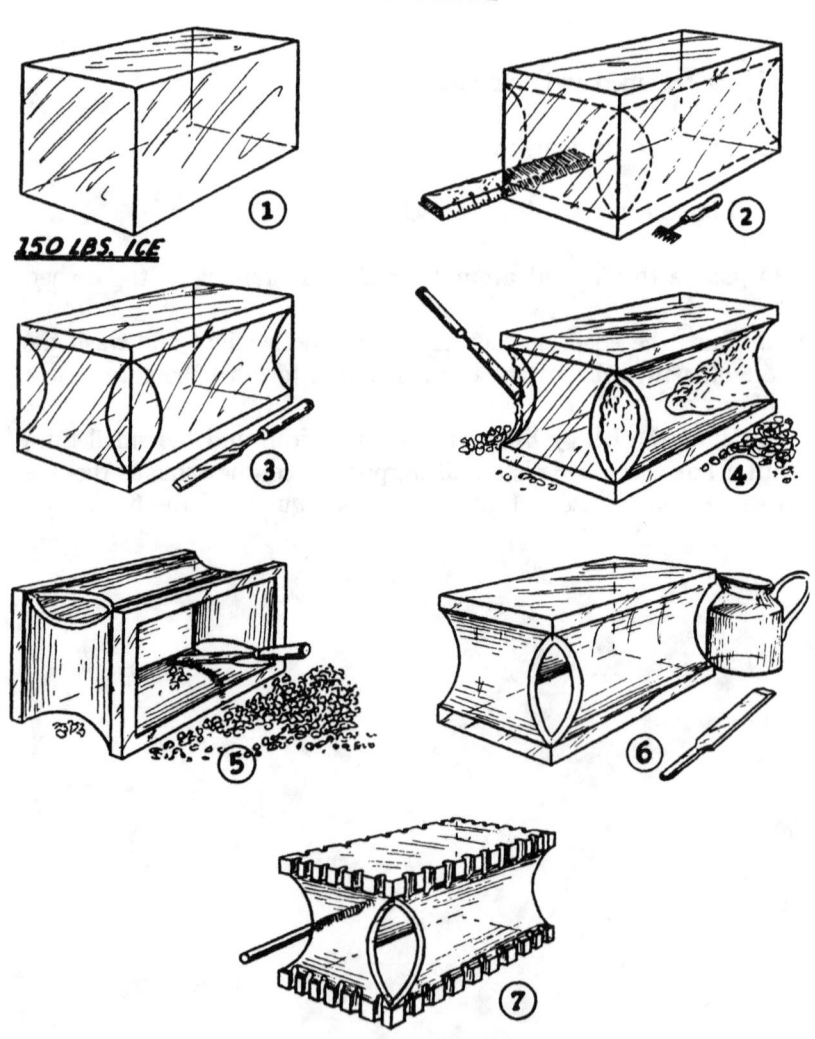

150 LBS. ICE

30

LOBSTER AND CRAB STAND

1. Ice trimmed and ready for use.

2. Ice correctly marked.

3. Lines deepened with V-chisel.

4. Carve ice out beginning at the corners as shown in diagram.

5. Place ice piece on the side and carve out the bottom as shown.

6. Piece correctly worked out.

7. Ice piece after lines are burned.

LESSON 10

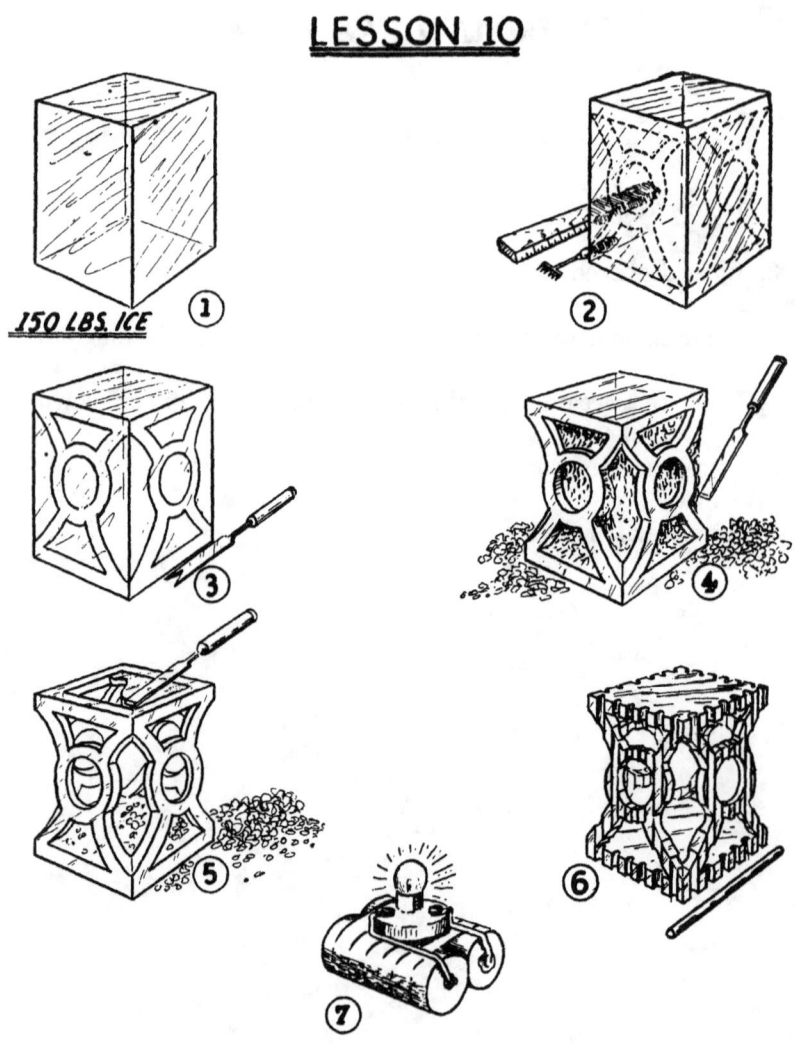

150 LBS. ICE ①

②

③

④

⑤

⑥

⑦

32

FANCY SANDWICH STAND

1. Ice trimmed and ready for use.

2. Ice correctly marked.

3. Lines deepened with V-chisel.

4. Starting on the corners, use one-inch chisel, carving three inches deep. Use a round chisel in the middle.

5. Turn the piece upside down and either carve or burn out the inside.

6. Bars may be round or flat and the lines burned in.

7. A small round piece of ice may be carved with a battery inserted. If this is placed inside the piece it gives an attractive effect.

LESSON 11

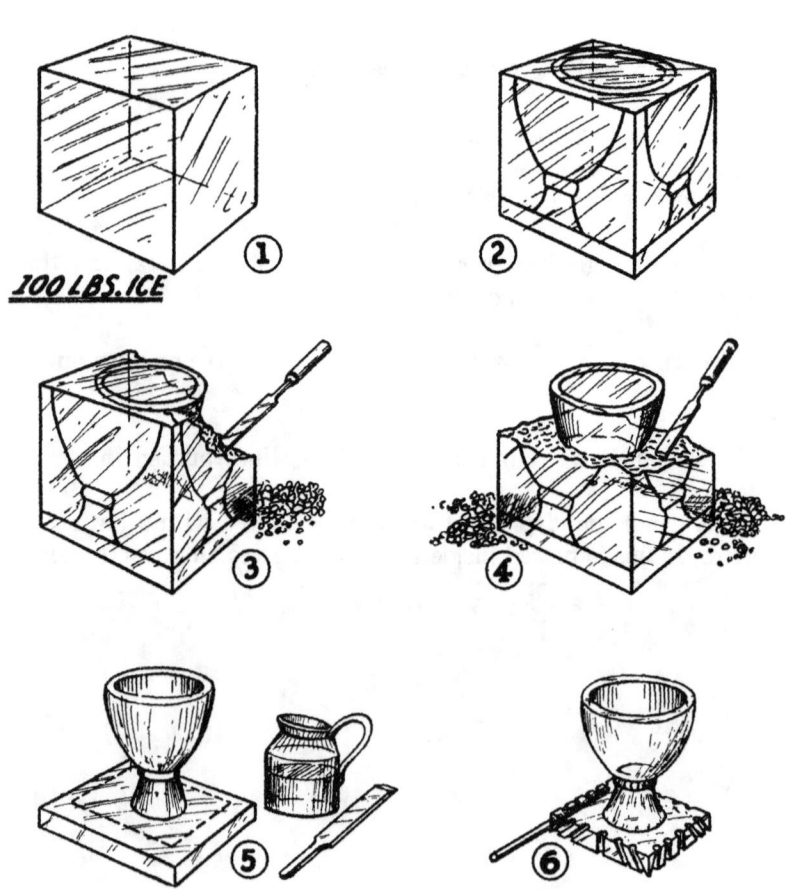

100 LBS. ICE

PLAIN CAVIAR BOWL

1. Ice trimmed and ready for use.

2. The ice is marked similar to method used in Lesson 5.

3. Use a two-inch chisel and, starting in one corner, keep working around the bowl.

4. This shows the piece half carved out.

5. Reduce the stand on which the bowl rests according to the size of the bowl. A stand that is too large detracts from the beauty of the piece.

6. Finished bowl with lines burned in.

This bowl is to be used for salads or caviar. Bowls may be made from larger pieces of ice and used to support punch bowls. In this case the punch bowl is inserted into the ice bowl in a similar manner to that in Lesson 5.

35

LESSON 12

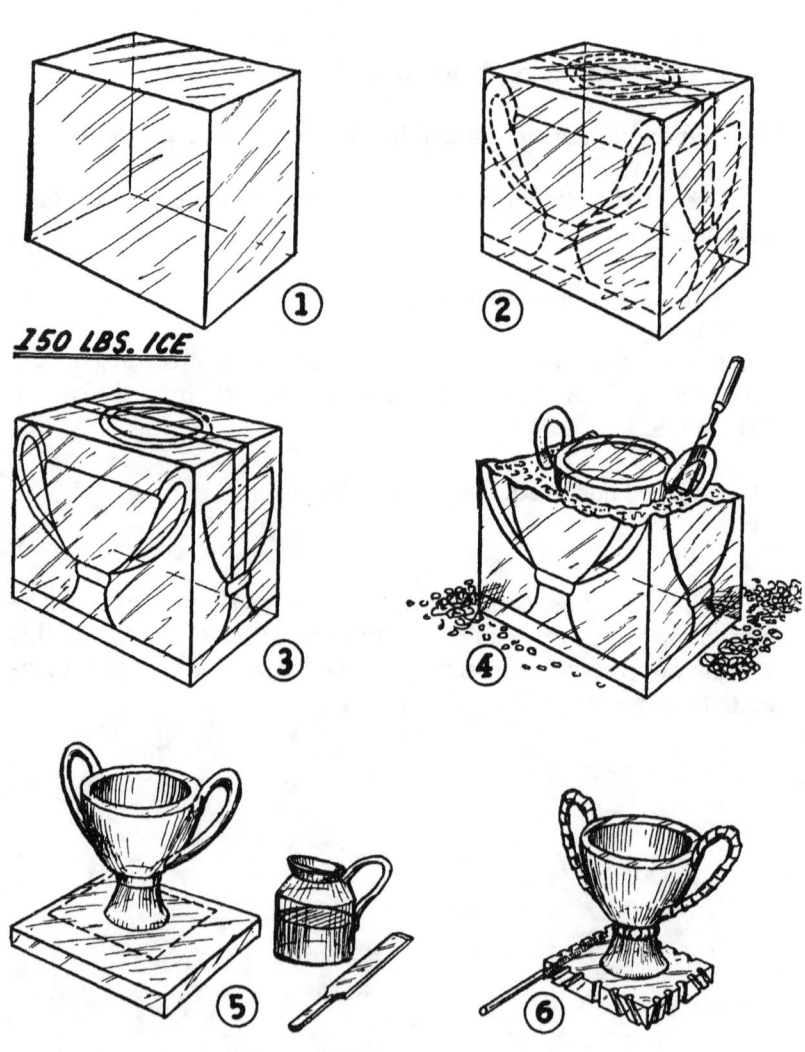

150 LBS. ICE

36

FANCY CAVIAR BOWL

1. Ice trimmed and ready for use.

2. Mark the design on top and on sides as shown.

3. Deepen lines with V-chisel and remove the part inside the circle on top to a depth of one and one-fourth inches. Leave the handle untouched.

4. Use the one-inch chisel and work carefully around the bowl from the top. For the handles, use the round chisel.

5. Remove the ice from the inside of the bowl and mark off the standard in proportion to the size of the bowl.

6. Completed bowl with raised handles and lines burned.

LESSON 13

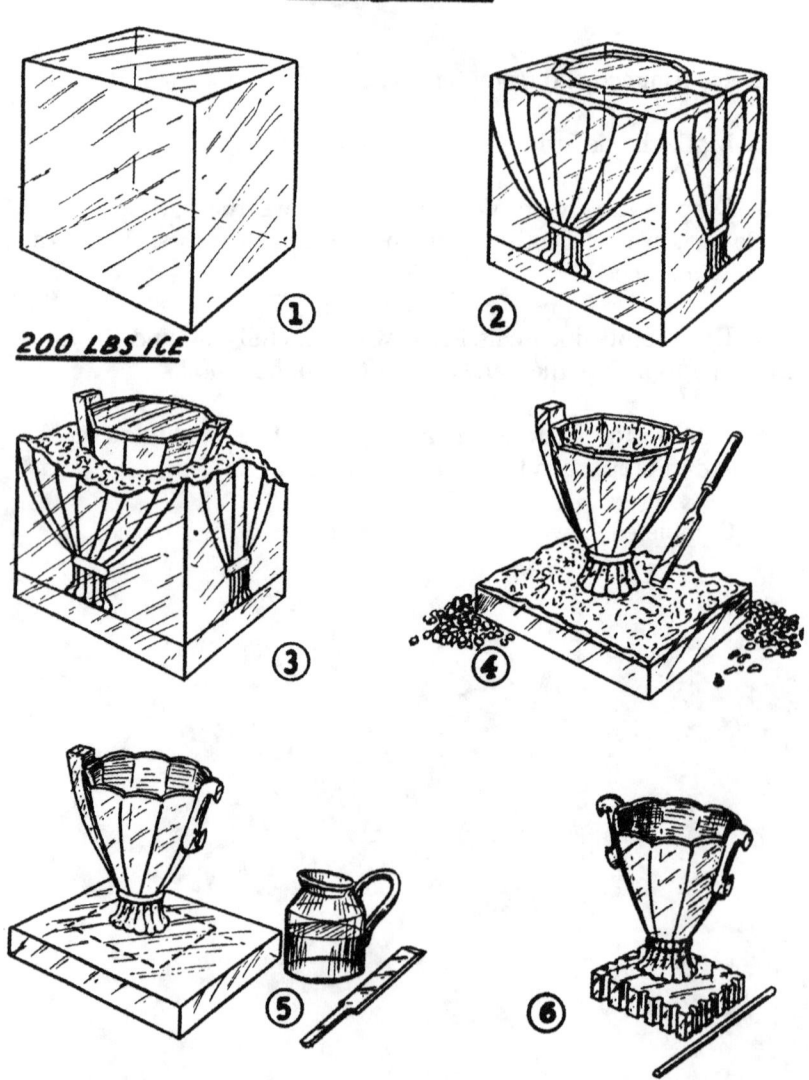

200 LBS ICE

① ② ③ ④ ⑤ ⑥

38

SHRIMP SALAD BOWL

1. Ice trimmed and ready for use.

2. Mark the design with the ice shaver.

3. Start at one corner and keep working around. Leave the middle of the bowl and the handles untouched. Chisel down halfway and inspect the piece thoroughly. If the proportions are out of balance, correction should be made at this time.

4. The bowl is now in the rough stage. The inside of the bowl and the handles have not yet been carved out. This must now be done very carefully, leaving the walls of the bowl one and one-half inches thick.

5. Wash off the shavings with cold water.

6. Burn deeper lines along the sides of the bowl and in the base and standard.

Very large bowls of this type are often used for punch bowls. They may be filled with fine cracked ice and a glass punch bowl inserted.

LESSON 14

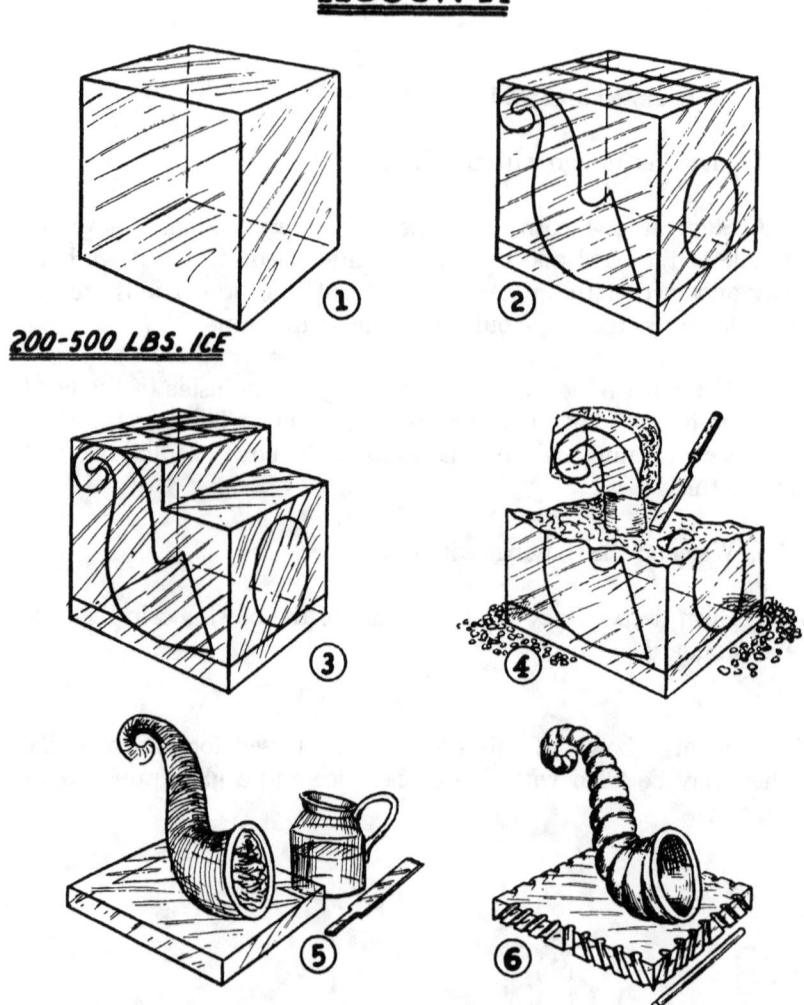

200-500 LBS. ICE

40

CORNUCOPIA

1. Ice trimmed and ready for use. The cornucopia or Horn of Plenty is a subject frequently used. It may be made of both small and large blocks of ice and may be filled with almost anything in the food line or with fresh flowers.

2. Mark the ice with ice shaver and chisel as shown.

3. The right half of the piece at the top is sawed off. Each outside third of the left half is also sawed off to a depth to correspond with the right half.

4. Leave the head of the horn rather thick and clumsy as indicated by the diagram until the whole horn is completed. Otherwise it would be melted down before the piece is finished.

5. Next remove the inside of the horn and finish cutting the head.

6. Deep lines should be burned around the horn as indicated. This piece is very effective when made of colored ice.

LESSON 15

300 LBS. ICE

① ② ③ ④ ⑤ ⑥

DECORATIVE FISH

1. Ice trimmed and ready for use.

2. Pattern of fish is marked on ice and lines marked for cutting away extra ice.

3. Left half, top of block, is sawed off down to just above top of fish pattern. The corners of the right half are sawed down to the same depth. You may then start carving the tail but do not finish it. Leave two more inches of ice around the tail than you will need. Otherwise, the tail will melt down before the piece is finished.

4. This shows how to carve around the fish. Do not carve the fins too thin.

5. Finish by carving the fish out with a good, sharp chisel. Carve out the base so that it may be used.

6. Lines may be burned into the fish, especially marking the fins. The base may be used for serving celery, salads, or caviar. This is especially good for fishing parties.

LESSON 16

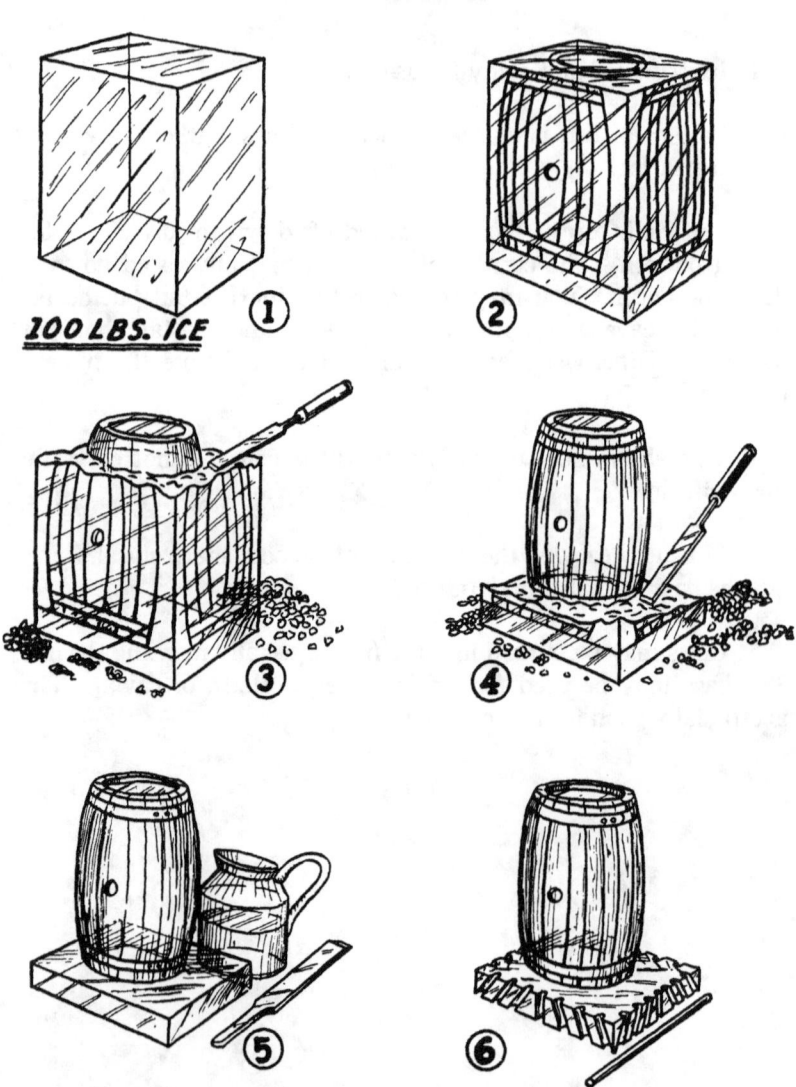

100 LBS. ICE ①

②

③

④

⑤

⑥

44

CAVIAR BARREL

1. Ice trimmed and ready to use.

2. Pattern marked on ice and lines ruled in for base.

3. Start at the top of the design with the two-inch chisel. Be sure to keep the design as you work down. Do not touch the inside ice.

4. The next step is to cut in the two bands, top and bottom of barrel. These are marked and the barrel around the bands is carved or burned so that the bands will stand out about three-fourths of an inch. Carve in the lines which represent the boards. The cork in the middle is raised one and one-half inch.

5. Finish by removing the inside ice. A bowl containing shrimp or caviar may be inserted. To get a perfect fit for the bowl you can insert it filled with hot water and let it sink into the inside of the barrel by itself.

6. Burn in the lines as indicated.

LESSON 17

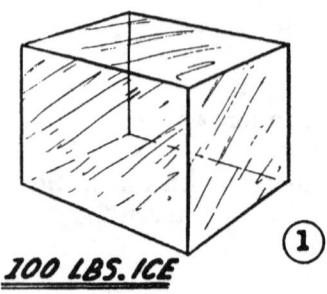

100 LBS. ICE ①

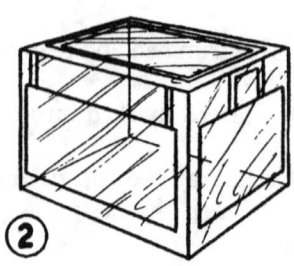

②

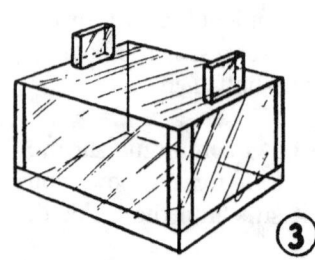

③

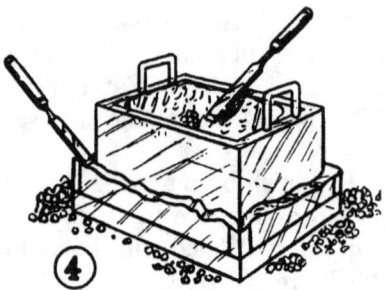

④

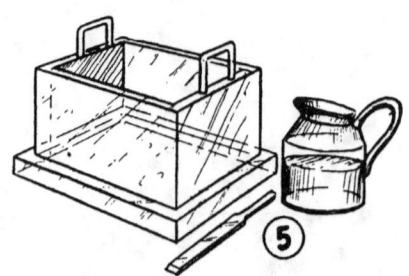

⑤

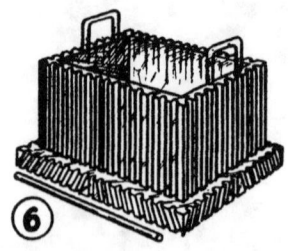

⑥

46

RELISH CONTAINER

1. Ice trimmed and ready for use.

2. Mark as indicated with ruler and ice shaver.

3. Start at the right-hand corner with the one-inch chisel, cutting along the top of the basket. If you cut down with your chisel your design will be straighter.

4. After you have carved out the basket down to the base, carve out the inside.

5. Wash off with cold water and, with a flat iron, burn the sides until they are straight and even.

6. Heat a round iron and burn deep lines into the basket and the base.

LESSON 18

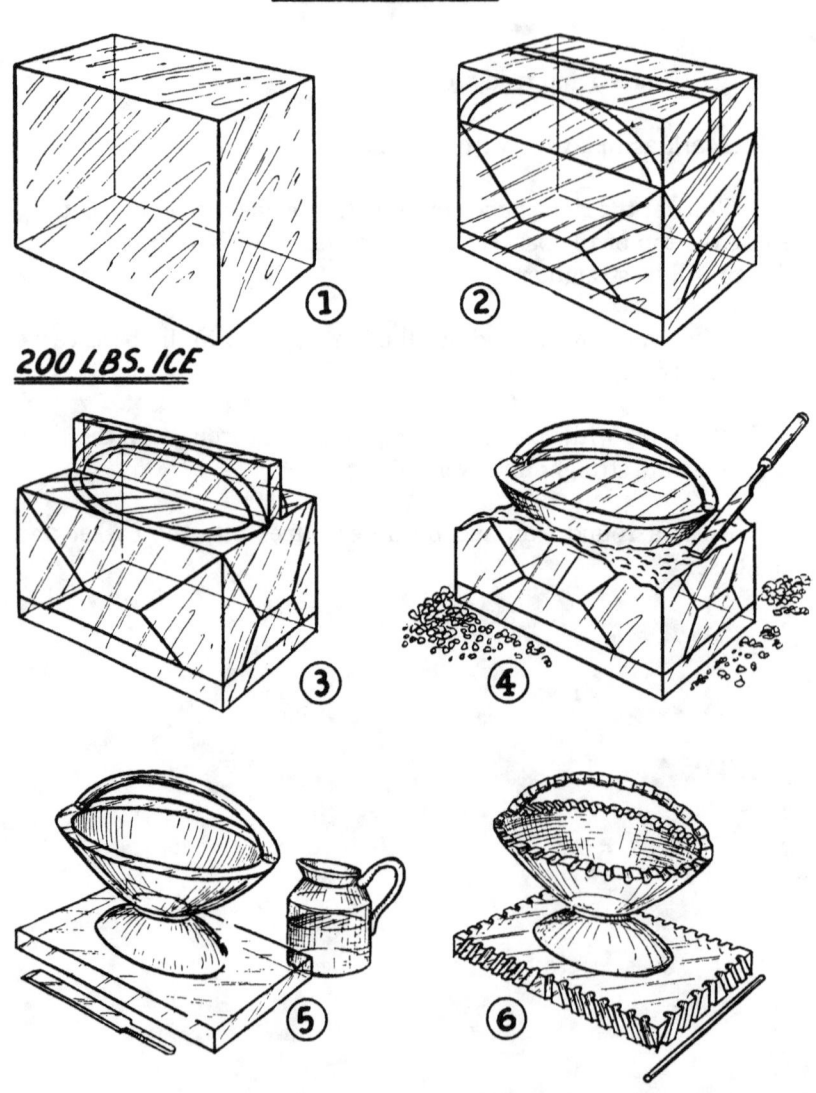

200 LBS. ICE

① ② ③ ④ ⑤ ⑥

48

FRUIT OR SALAD BASKET

1. Ice trimmed and ready for use.

2. Mark as indicated.

3. Saw away the top part of each side, leaving the ice for the handle intact. This piece must be marked again with the shaver to get it absolutely even. The handle should be about four inches thick.

4. Start with the chisel at one corner, removing the ice from the outside of the basket until you reach the base. Remove the ice from inside but only part of the way down as indicated by the dotted line. Now chisel out the handle. This is done last to prevent melting.

5. Wash off with cold water.

6. Burn the lines in the handle, basket, and base. When food is served in this basket, the inside is filled with fine cracked ice on which a platter of food is placed.

LESSON 19

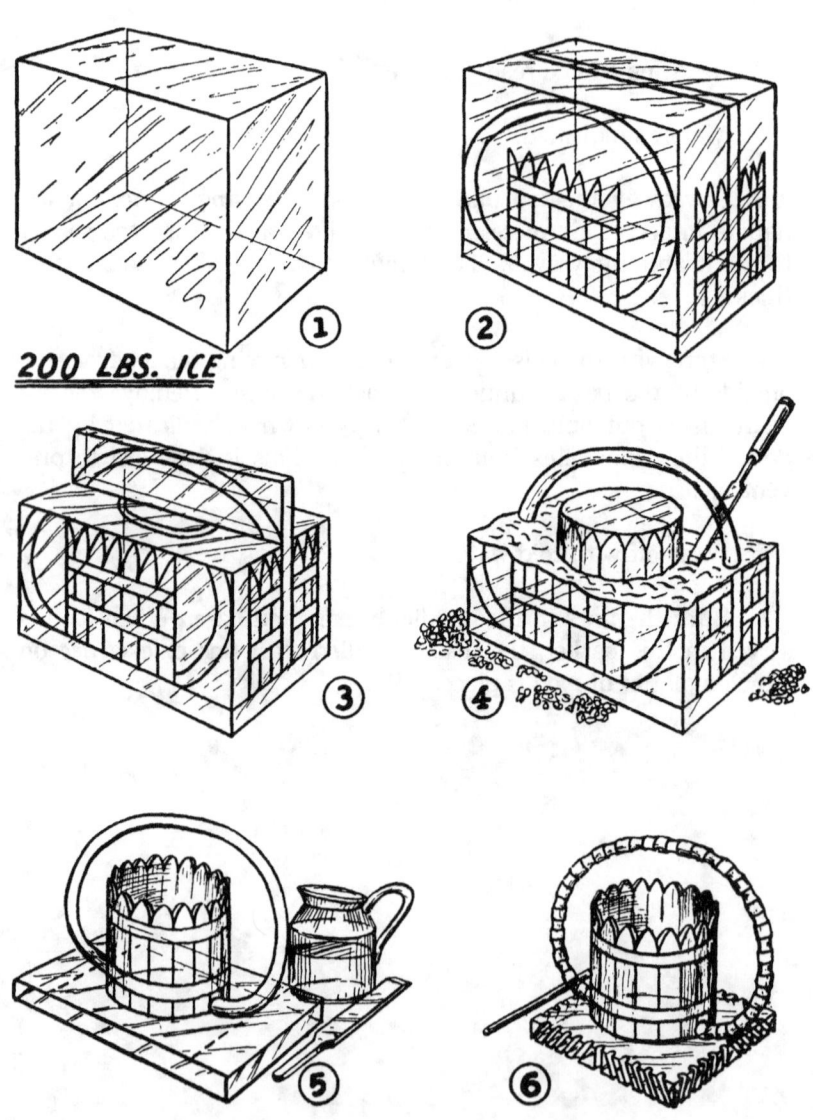

200 LBS. ICE

① ② ③ ④ ⑤ ⑥

SHRIMP BASKET

1. Ice trimmed and ready for use.

2. Mark pattern with ruler and chisel as indicated.

3. Saw down from the top, as indicated for handles in previous lesson. Leave ice four inches thick for the handle and re-mark it to get right proportion.

4. Start at one corner and work your way around the basket and handle.

5. Do not cut out balance of handle until basket is completed.

6. After basket is washed and well rounded, burn it with a round iron to give it the effect of logs.

LESSON 20

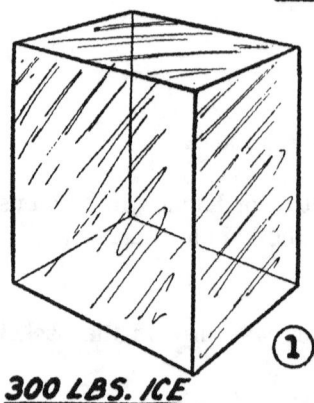

(1)

300 LBS. ICE

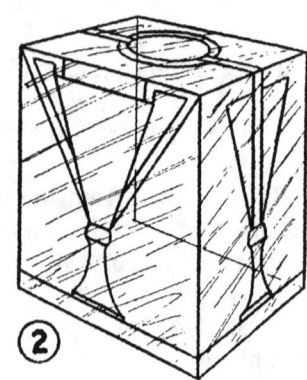

(2)

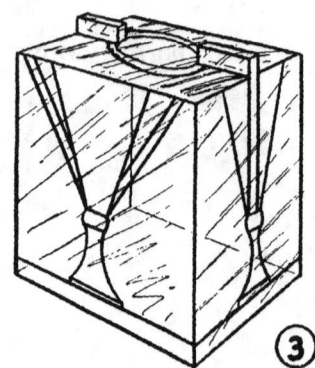

(3)

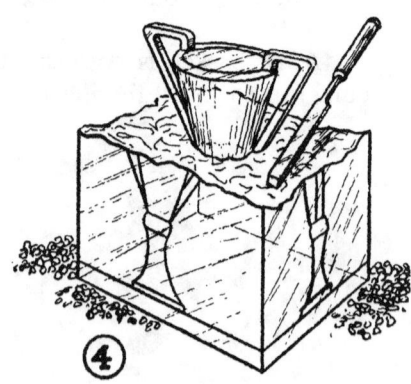

(4)

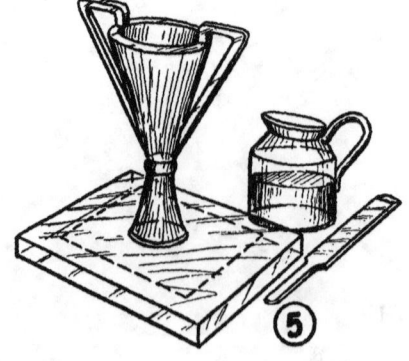

(5)

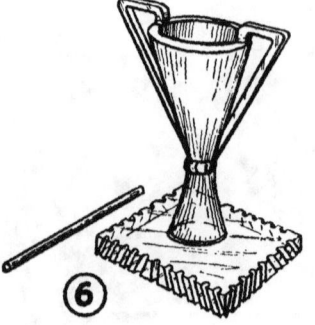

(6)

52

TROPHY

1. Ice trimmed and ready for use.

2. Mark with ruler and chisel. Trophies, to be effective, must be of good size which means using 200 to 300 pounds of ice. The larger the piece, the more exacting one must be in the trimming and marking.

3. The handles are partly sawed out on top after which the ice is chiseled away along the sides of the trophy. Leave the handles until the last.

4. When making larger pieces, it is advisable to check them constantly to make sure that they are even. It is easy to tilt such pieces in carving. A level may be used for this. In carving handles, use a sharp chisel and delicate strokes or burn them with a flat hot iron.

5. The inside of the trophy should be burned out.

6. Lines are burned only on the base. After the piece is finished, place it in the cooler to regain firmness.

LESSON 21

300 LBS. ICE

DECORATED TROPHY

1. Ice trimmed and ready for use.

2. Exact trimming and marking is particularly necessary.

3. Carve around the bowl and the handles from top to bottom. Leave the ice inside the bowl and inside the handles.

4. After the ice is removed from the outside and the trophy appears well-balanced and in proportion, cut out the handles and last, the inside of the bowl.

5. Burn in the lines and the design as indicated.

6. Burn the lines in the base and place in a cooler until ready for use.

LESSON 22

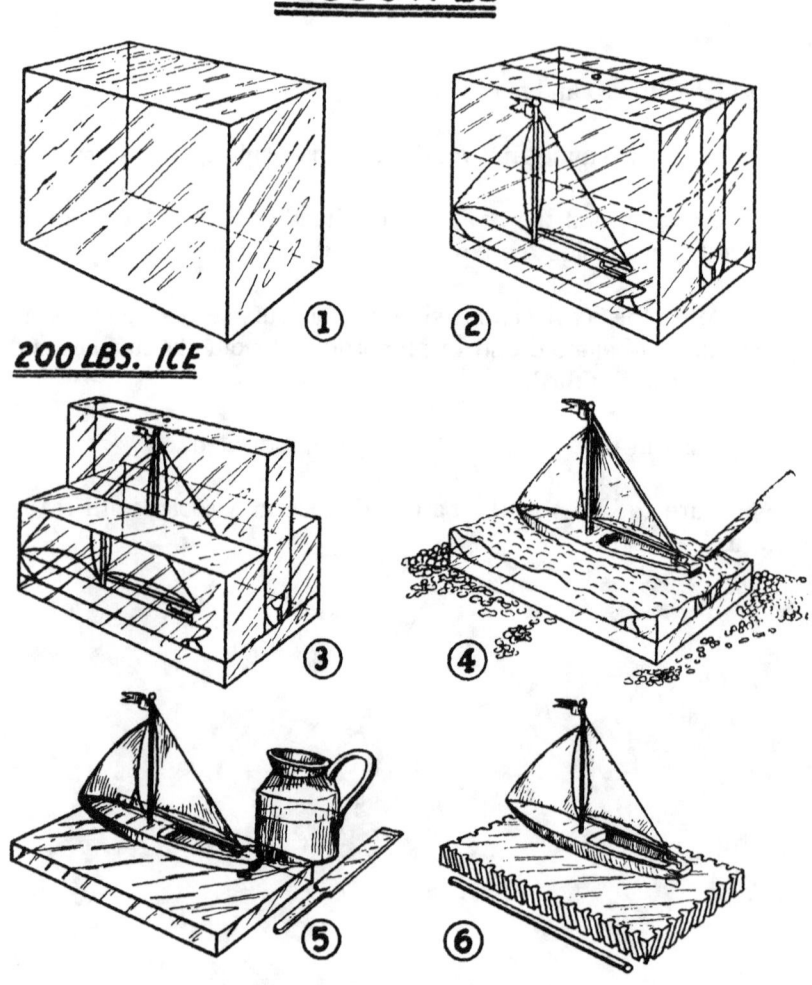

① ② ③ ④ ⑤ ⑥

200 LBS. ICE

56

SAIL BOAT

1. Ice trimmed and ready for use.

2. Mark carefully indicating the ship as well as the ice to be sawed away.

3. Saw along the lines as indicated and mark in the sail once more.

4. Carve the sail roughly and not too thin.

5. Carve the entire boat. Finish the sails, making them thinner and smoother.

6. If the base is hollowed out from the bottom and an electric battery with a blue light placed in the hollow spot, it gives the effect of the boat on water.

LESSON 23

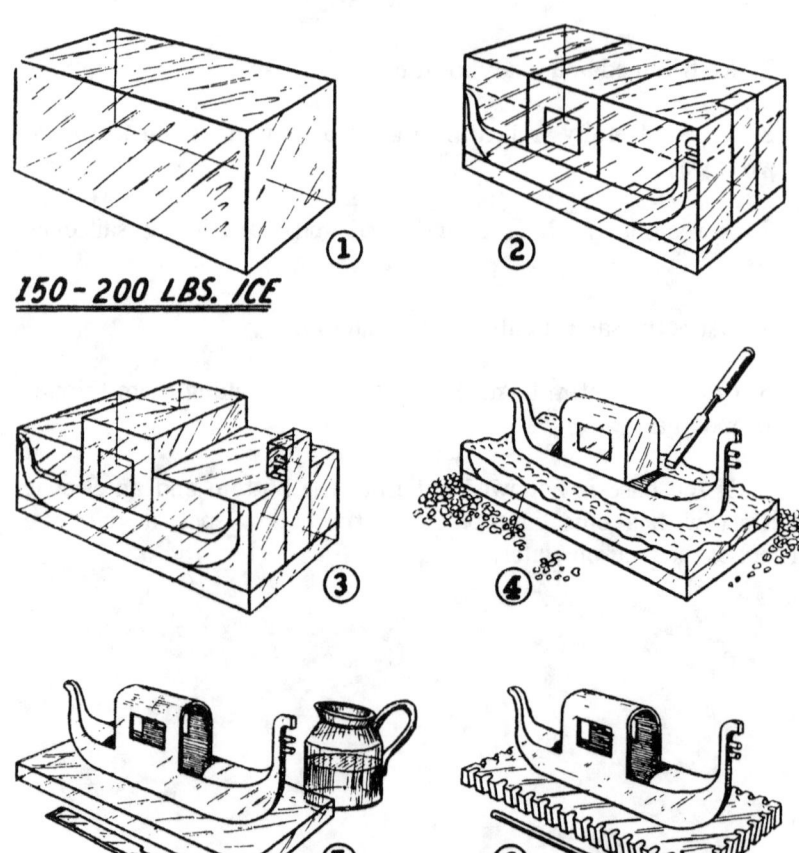

150 - 200 LBS. ICE

① ② ③ ④ ⑤ ⑥

GONDOLA

1. Ice trimmed and ready for use.

2. Marked with ruler and shaver. Lines deepened with V-chisel.

3. Saw out the extra ice as indicated down to the dotted line. Start to carve the middle of the gondola and leave the ends until the last.

4. When the entire boat is carved out, hollow out the canopy, leaving it about one inch thick. Also carve out the ends.

5. Burn in any design with a hot iron and wash with cold water.

6. These are used mostly for show pieces. They may be used for small canapes.

LESSON 24

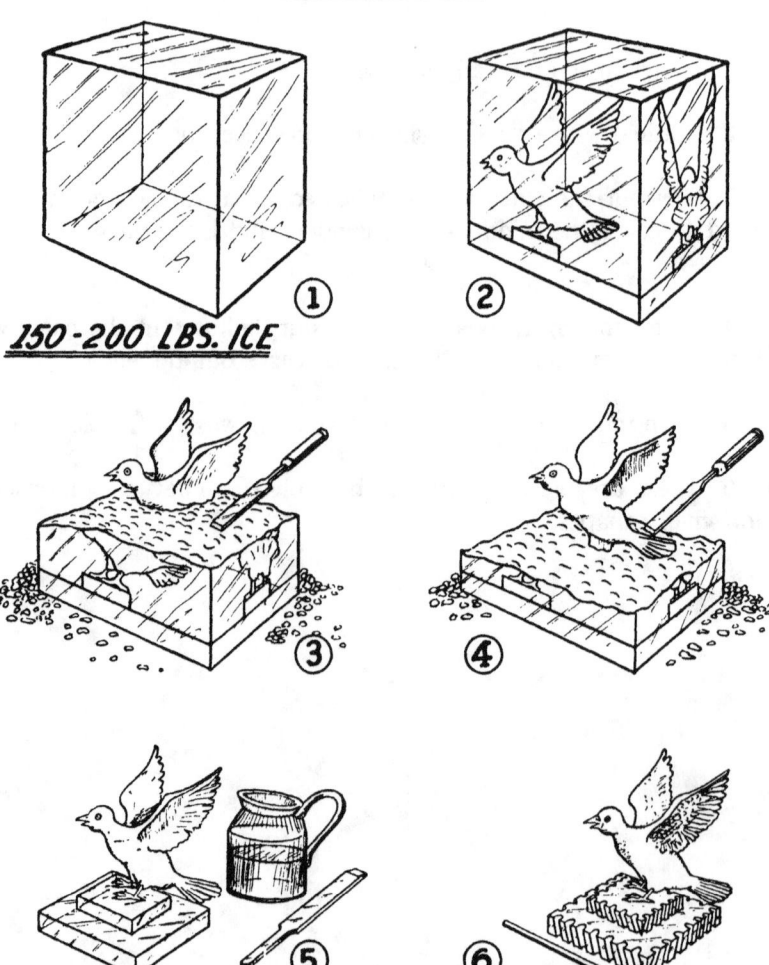

150-200 LBS. ICE

① ② ③ ④ ⑤ ⑥

DOVE CENTER PIECE

1. Ice trimmed and ready for use.

2. Mark in the bird carefully.

3. Carve from the top, cutting out the wings and head first. These are carved roughly at the start leaving plenty of ice around them for melting.

4. Carve out the base and make sure that it is level. It is best to measure the sides with a ruler. Finish the wings and the head.

5. Carve the lines in the wings. Do not burn them in.

6. Burn deep lines into the bottom base, lighter ones on the top. This piece is used mostly as a decorative center piece. It may be carved from 400 pounds of ice also.

LESSON 25

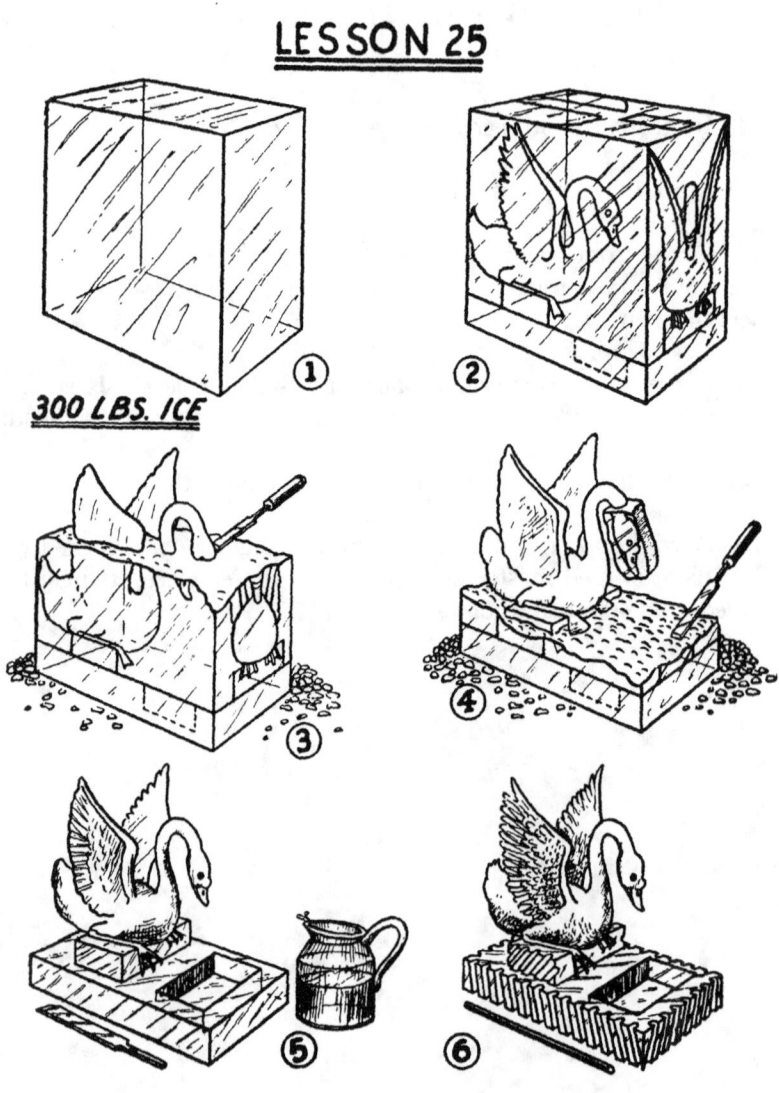

300 LBS. ICE

SWAN CENTER PIECE

1. Ice trimmed and ready for use.

2. Swans are carved more than any other bird. They are not so difficult to make as some of the others. Many students do a perfect job the first time they attempt this piece. Proper trimming and exact marking is eighty per cent of the reason for good results.

3. Carve out the wing tips and the top of the neck first. Gradually chisel down. Do not, at this stage, carve the lines on the bird. Just give it the general outline as is seen in figures 3 and 4.

4. When the outline is roughly carved, carve the feathers into the wings and finish the bottom base.

5. Finish the swan's head, giving light gentle strokes with a sharp chisel. It is better to burn the head in if care is taken not to burn too much. Wash off with cold water.

6. Lines may be burned into the base and the birds as one wishes. This piece may be used for any occasion.

LESSON 26

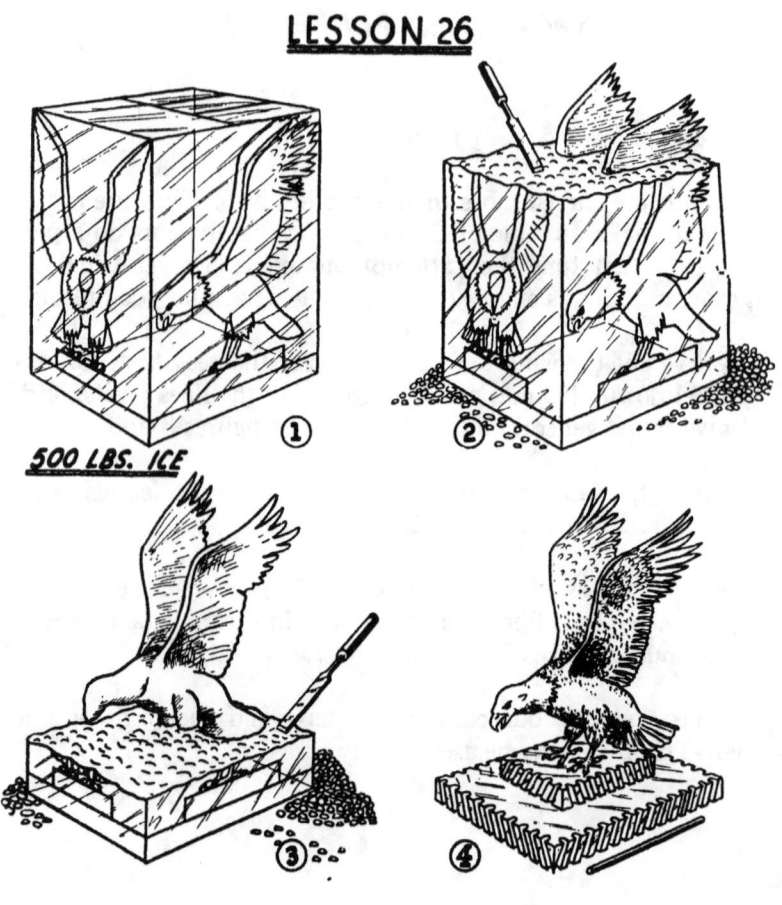

500 LBS. ICE

① ② ③ ④

EAGLE CENTER PIECE

1. Ice trimmed and marked. Make sure the ice is level and that the markings are clear.

2. Carve the wing tips first down to the place marked with an "X" or deeper—to where the body meets the wings. This is about even with the head. Next cut out the head and form the body. Leave plenty of ice on all to be carved out later.

3. Now check position of the bird. If needed, make corrections at this point. Carve out bird with tail spread, and the base. Carve the feathers and claws and head with a well rounded beak.

4. Burn in the eyes and some of the feathers but be careful not to burn too deeply. This is strictly a center piece. Use large pieces of ice.

LESSON 27

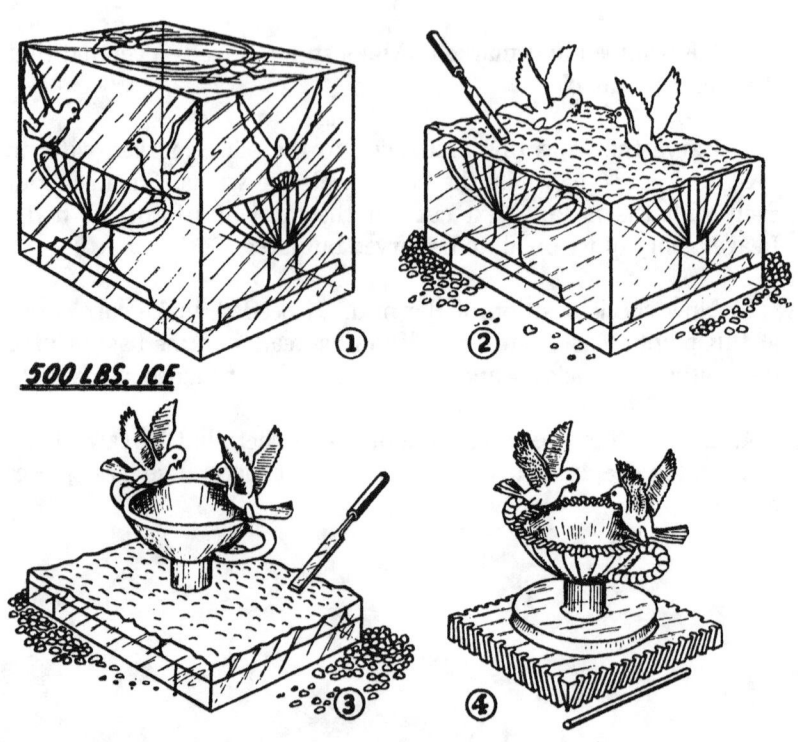

500 LBS. ICE

① ② ③ ④

66

TWIN DOVE SALAD BOWL

1. Four hundred pounds of ice are needed for this piece and it requires precision work, speed, and exact calculation. Beginners should not try to make this piece until they have had complete results with previous pieces. To make one bird is comparatively easy but to make another the same size is many times more difficult.

2. Carve the wing tips on both birds quite thickly. Work on down the piece, chiseling evenly all around as indicated. When the bowl is reached, check the work constantly and make corrections as they seem necessary. Carve out the bowl but leave the inside ice until later.

3. Cut the base in proportion to the size of the bowl. Remove the inside ice from the bowl, cut in the feathers and finish off the heads last.

4. Burn the lines into the bowl and place the piece into the cooler to harden. It is a fine center piece. Salad or caviar may be served in the bowl.

LESSON 28

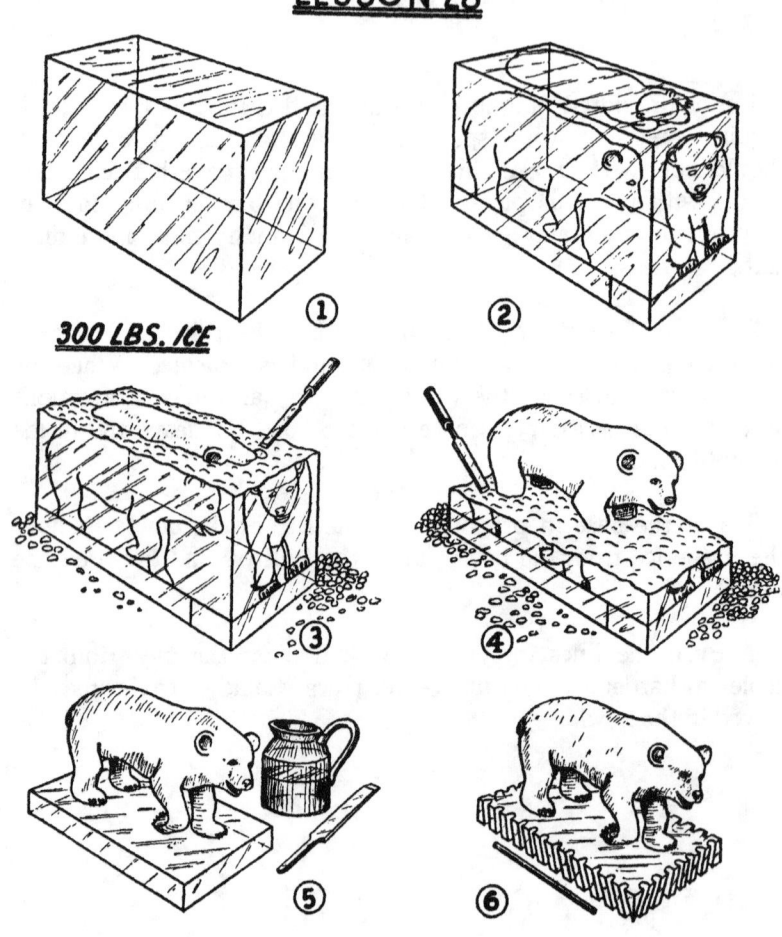

300 LBS. ICE

① ② ③ ④ ⑤ ⑥

BEAR CENTER PIECE

1. Ice trimmed and ready to use.

2. Carved ice animals are in great demand but they are more difficult to make which is the reason they are not used so often. Those that stand on four legs melt away more rapidly and they must be kept in coolers. The bear may be made in any position— standing, sitting, standing on its hind legs, or lying on its back. If you have a deep base the bear's back will reach almost to the top of the cake and you have little ice to take off. Otherwise, you can take off several inches.

3. Carve the ears out first, then the top of the body and chisel on down.

4. Carve out the entire bear and the base.

5. Cut a few wrinkles into the bear's body and head and wash all with cold water.

6. Burn lines in the base and hollow it out for the insertion of a battery with a green bulb.

LESSON 29

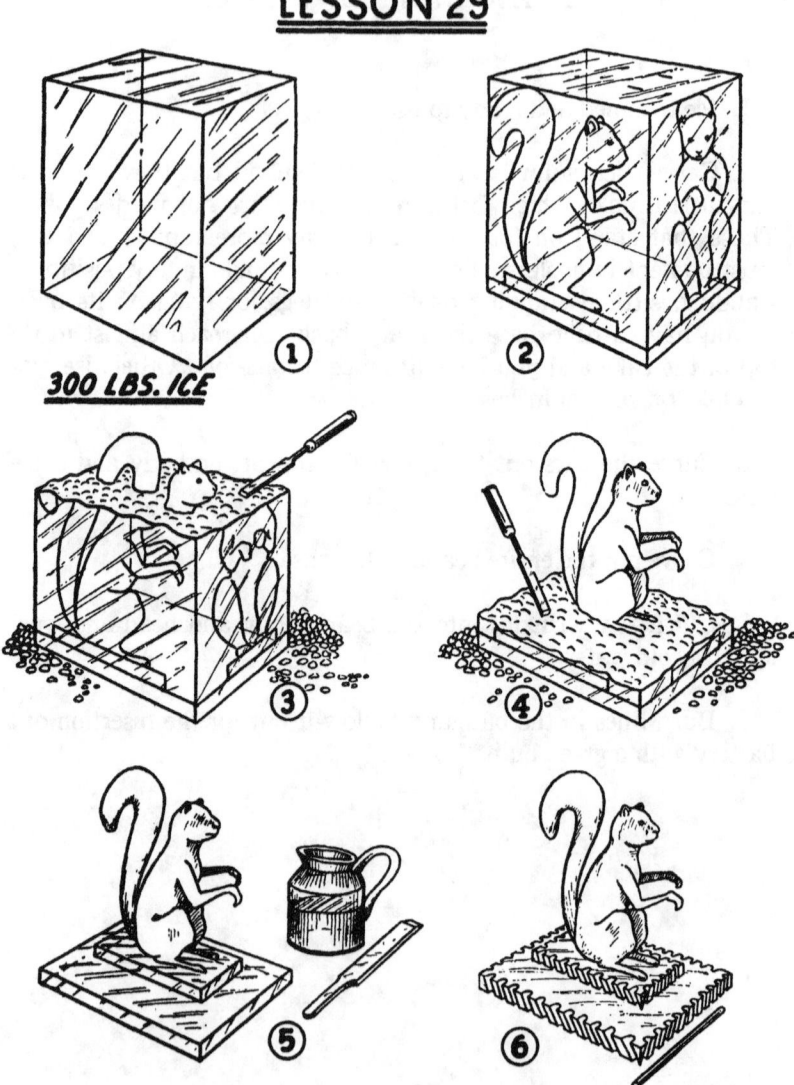

300 LBS. ICE

SQUIRREL CENTER PIECE

1. Ice trimmed and ready for use.

2. The sitting squirrel is very attractive in ice and not particularly difficult to make. Even 200 pounds of ice will make a squirrel of good size. Mark the design with care.

3. First cut out the ears, head, and the top of the tail and continue carving down.

4. Carve the animal out first and the base last.

5. Burn some lines in the tail, body, and claws as indicated.

6. Burn lines in the base.

LESSON 30

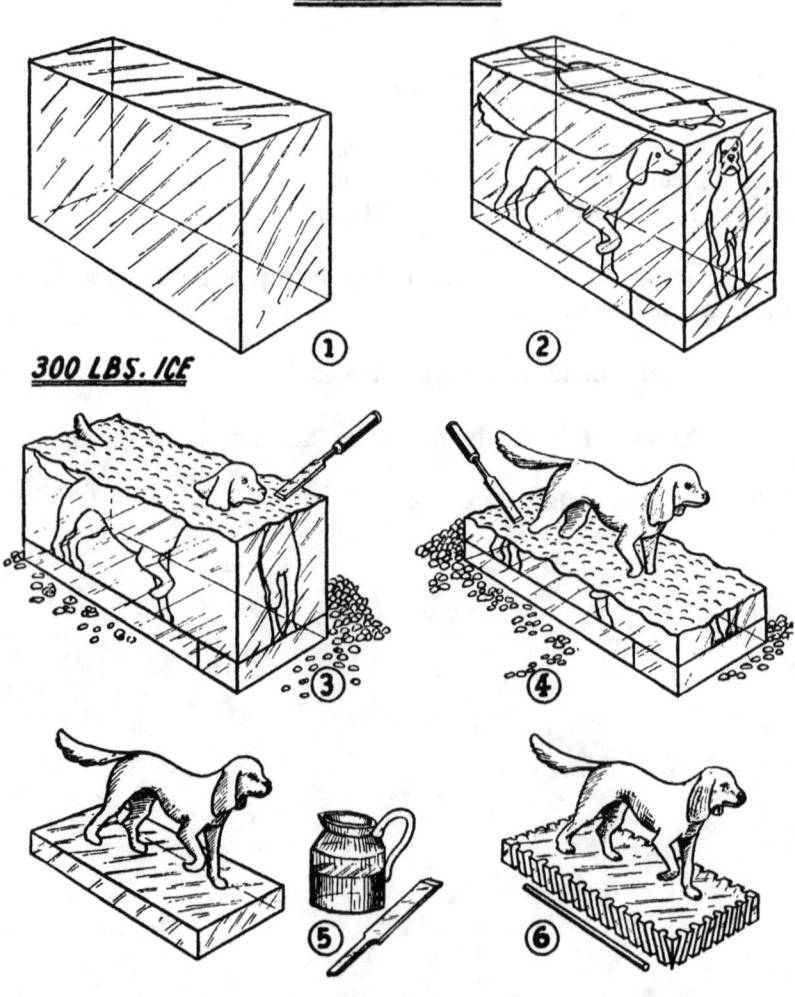

300 LBS. ICE

① ② ③ ④ ⑤ ⑥

72

HUNTING DOG CENTER PIECE

1. Ice trimmed and ready for use.

2. The dog is a great favorite in ice although not such an easy subject. A dog may be carved in several positions. Be sure the ice is level and the design well marked.

3. Cut the head out first, gradually cutting deeper along the neck. Keep carving down until you get to the legs. Here you cut straight down till you come to the base.

4. Carefully carve the body, head, and neck in proportion. Cut the legs out carefully and carve out the base.

5. Burn lines into the tail, ears, and body. Wash with cold water.

6. Burn lines into the base. If it seems advisable to give the piece support, a tree or stump may be added on one side.

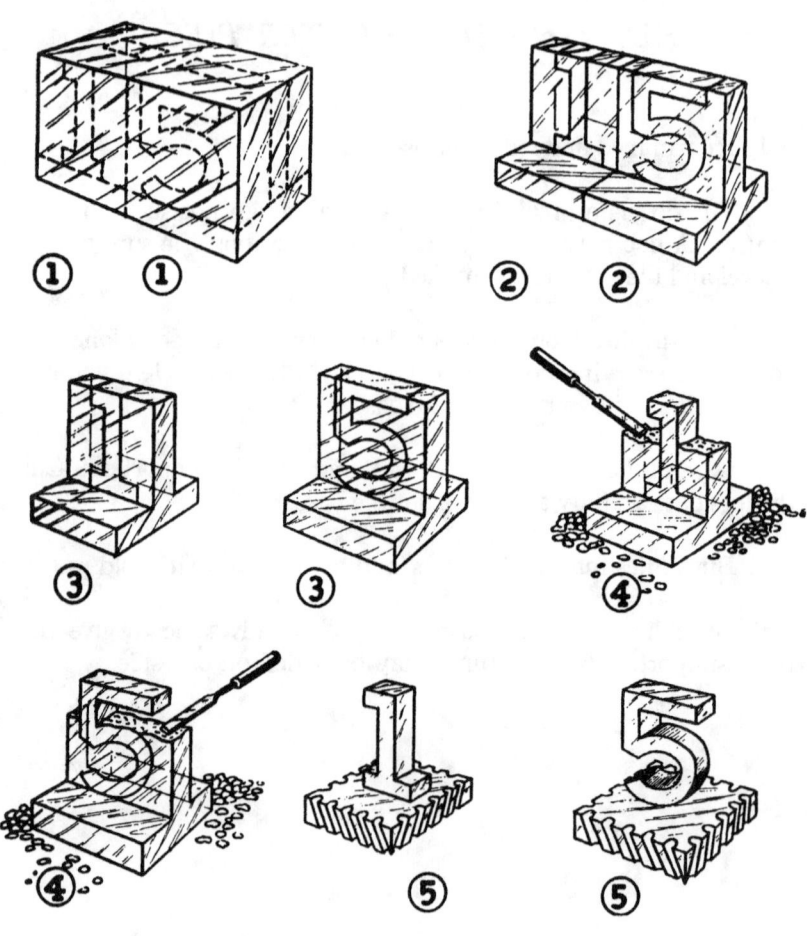

74

NUMBERS AND LETTERS IN ICE

Numbers and letters are often required to be carved out of natural or colored ice. They may be used for birthdays, holidays, or other celebrations. Sometimes entire sentences may be made. Often two or more characters may be carved out of one piece of ice.

The important thing to keep in mind is exactness of measurement. They must be the same height and thickness. One letter or figure that is out of alignment may necessitate remaking an entire group.

Numbers and letters should not be less than five inches thick. If many characters are required, place each one as it is completed in a cooler at five degrees below zero. They may be kept several weeks in this way. If they are to be colored they may be sprayed in the low temperature cooler with colored water and a fine spray.

Molds may be made of these characters and later filled with water and frozen. This saves a great deal of time and assures uniform appearance. In addition, the ice pieces may later be made by an inexperienced cook. The molds are well worth the investment as they will last indefinitely if handled carefully.

NUMBERS

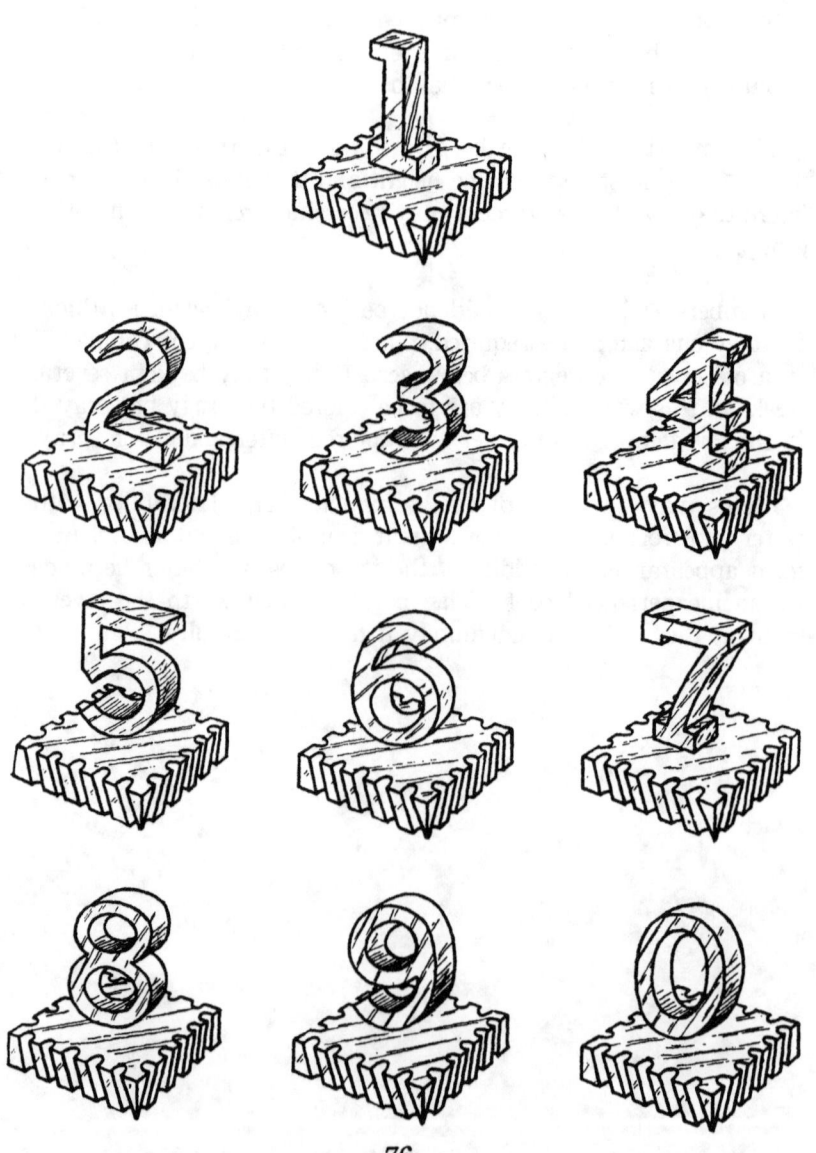

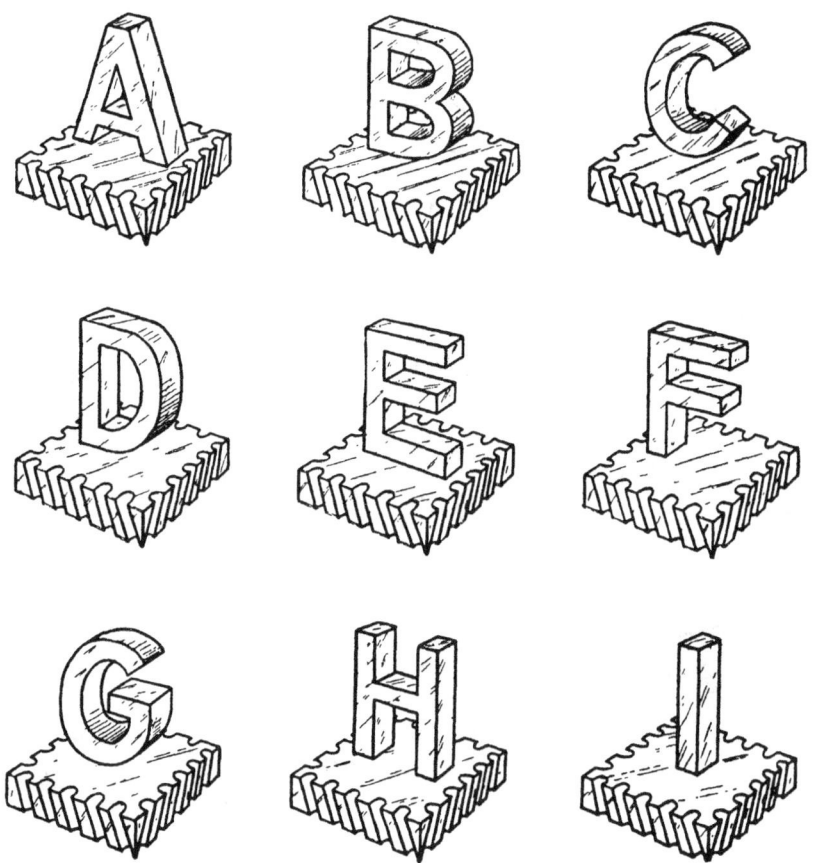

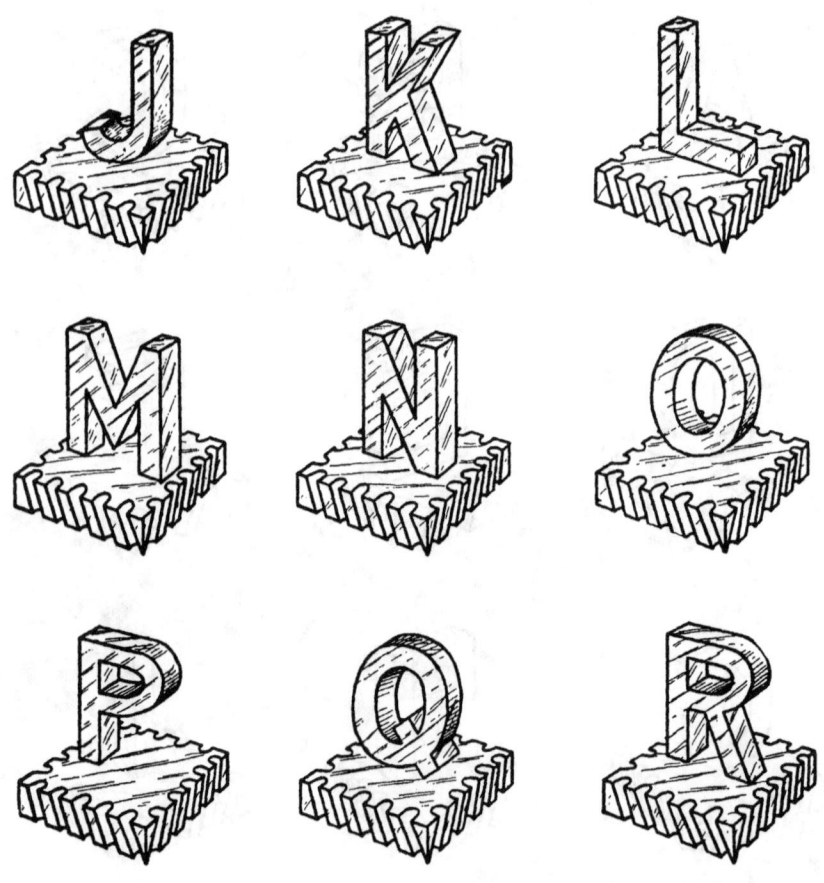

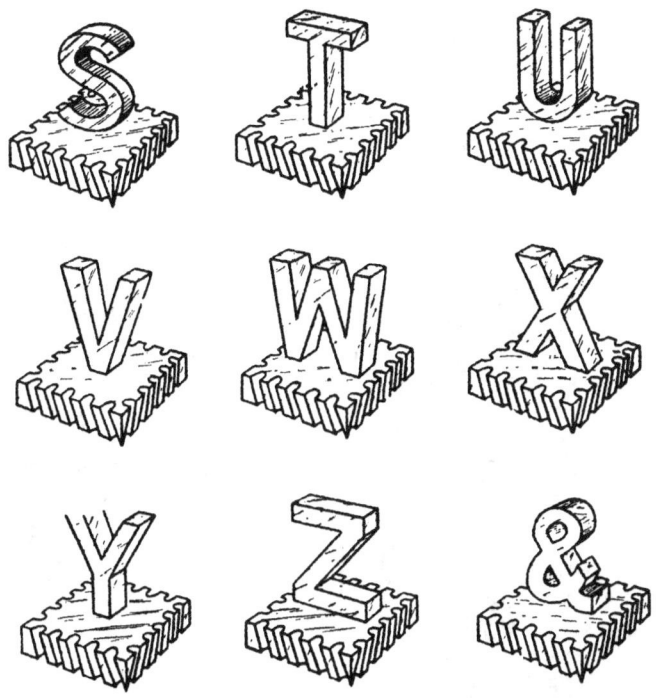

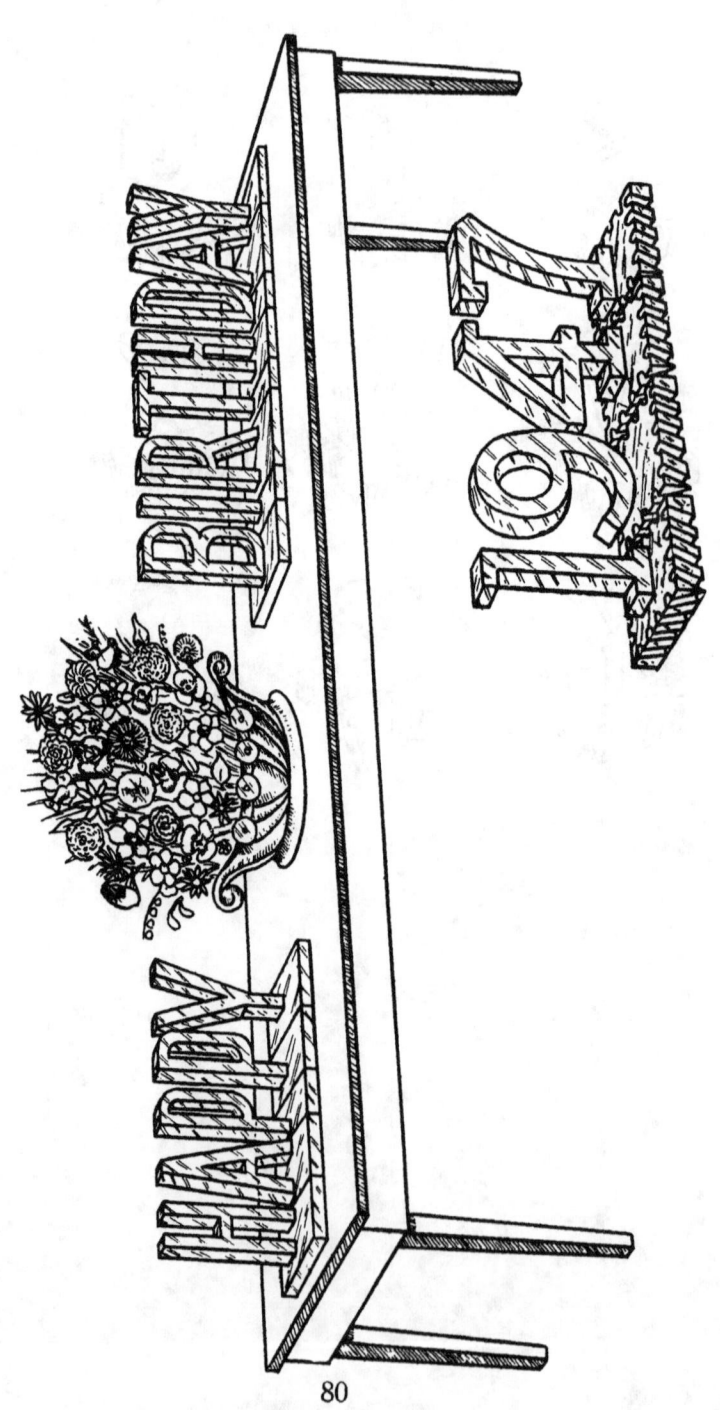

LETTERS AND NUMBERS

This illustrates the effectiveness of many letters and numbers used together. Many combinations are used—Good Luck, Good Health, Happy Days, Bon Voyage—and the name of the person for whom the party is given may also be added to any of the above.

When many letters and numbers are to be carved they should be started several days ahead of the date on which they are to be used. Molds would be a great help. When the letters or figures in the molds are frozen hard, they may be removed by running hot water over the molds. Colored water may be used to make the characters or they may be sprayed with colored water after they are finished.

HORSE

This is a difficult piece to make because of the delicate legs. If they are made in advance of use they must be placed in a cooler with the temperature well below zero. It will lessen the risk considerably if the piece is braced against a tree stump.

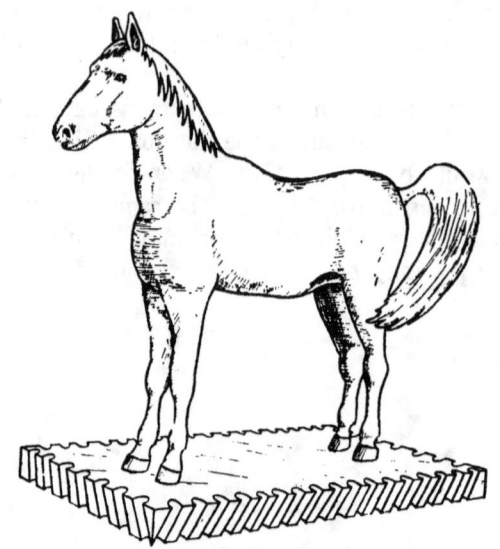

TURTLE

The turtle may be made from ice colored green and the base from ice colored blue. The piece may be hollowed out from below and a battery and colored light placed inside.

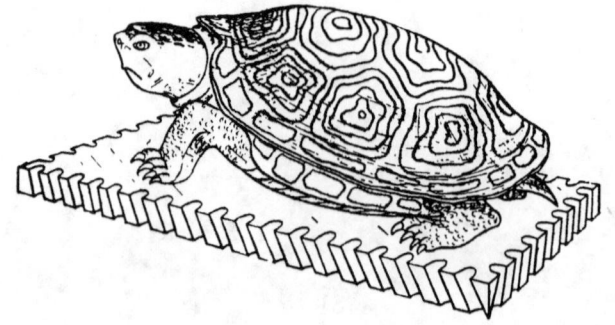

MOUNTAIN LION

This piece may assume unlimited poses—sitting, crouching, lying, or playing. The legs are heavier and sturdier than those of other animals.

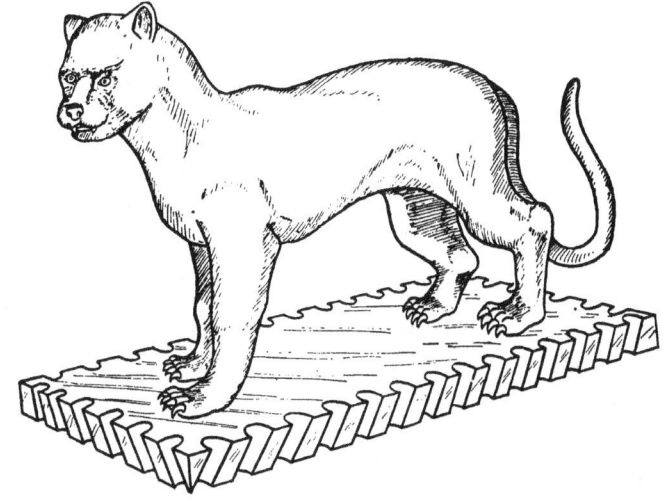

RABBIT

The legs of the rabbit in this position are very thin and it is advisable to give them the added support of a tree or stump.

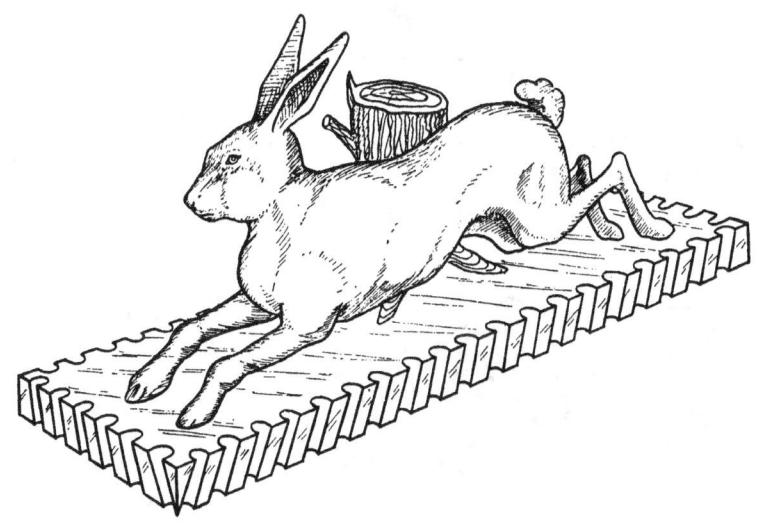

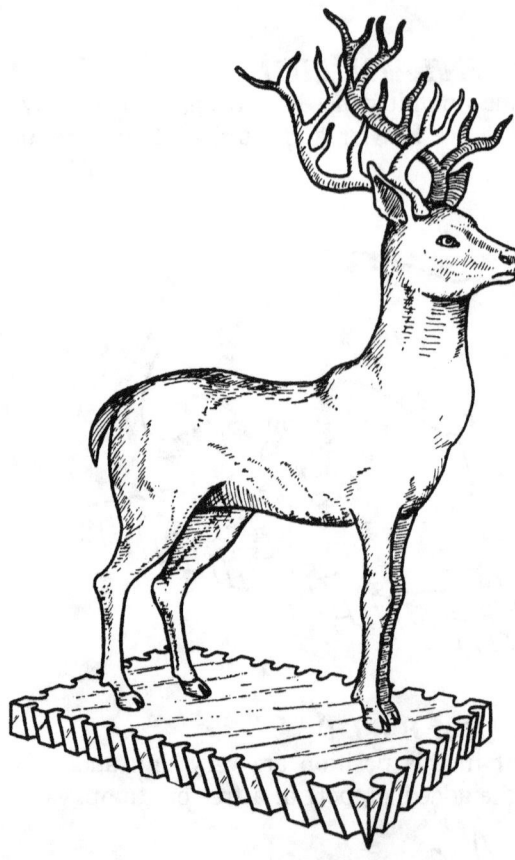

DEER

This is a difficult piece to make. Carve out the antlers first but leave plenty of ice around them and finish them last. After the body is finished, burn the antlers down to their proper size and place the piece in the cooler.

ALLIGATOR

The teeth are the most difficult part of this piece and must be carefully burned in with the aid of a thin hot iron. Place in a cooler unless used immediately after completion.

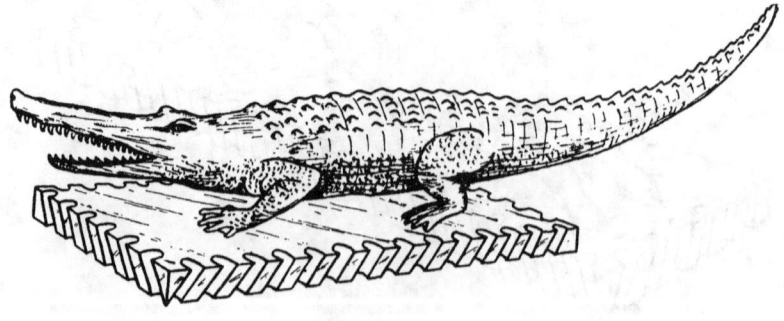

LION

The lion is not difficult to make provided the proportions are correct. If the mouth is open, the teeth must be burned in with great care.

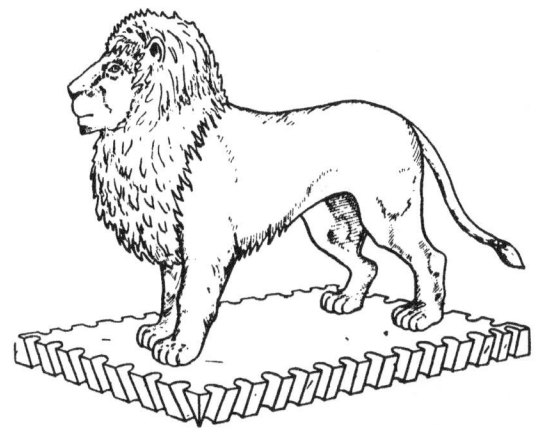

ELEPHANT

The elephant is not so difficult to make. The tusks should be made last and burned in with a hot iron.

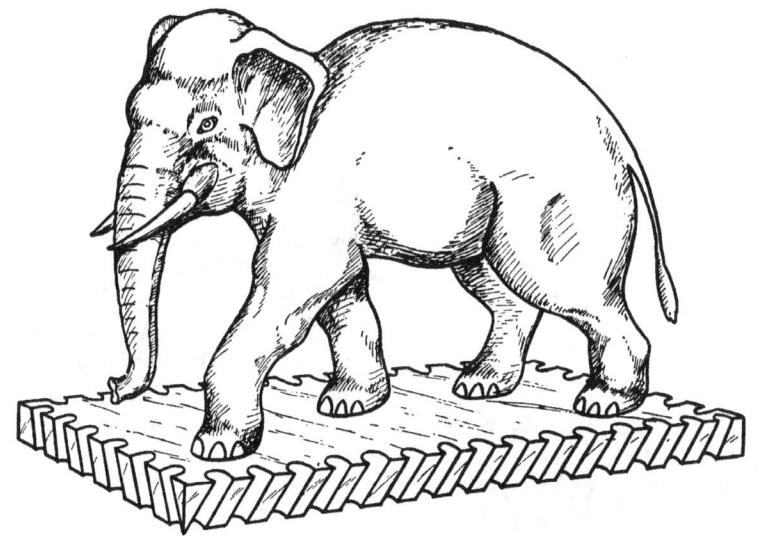

FRUIT SALAD BOWL

This piece may be made from three pieces of ice. When each is completed they are placed one on top of the other, placed in a cooler overnight and in the morning they will be frozen together. Fruit may be placed in these bowls, on top of napkins so that it does not come in contact with the ice. They may also be used for salads and hors d'oeuvres. Since this is a large piece there is bound to be more or less water dripping from it as the ice melts. It should stand in some sort of a container in which a white cloth is loosely folded to catch the dripping from the ice.

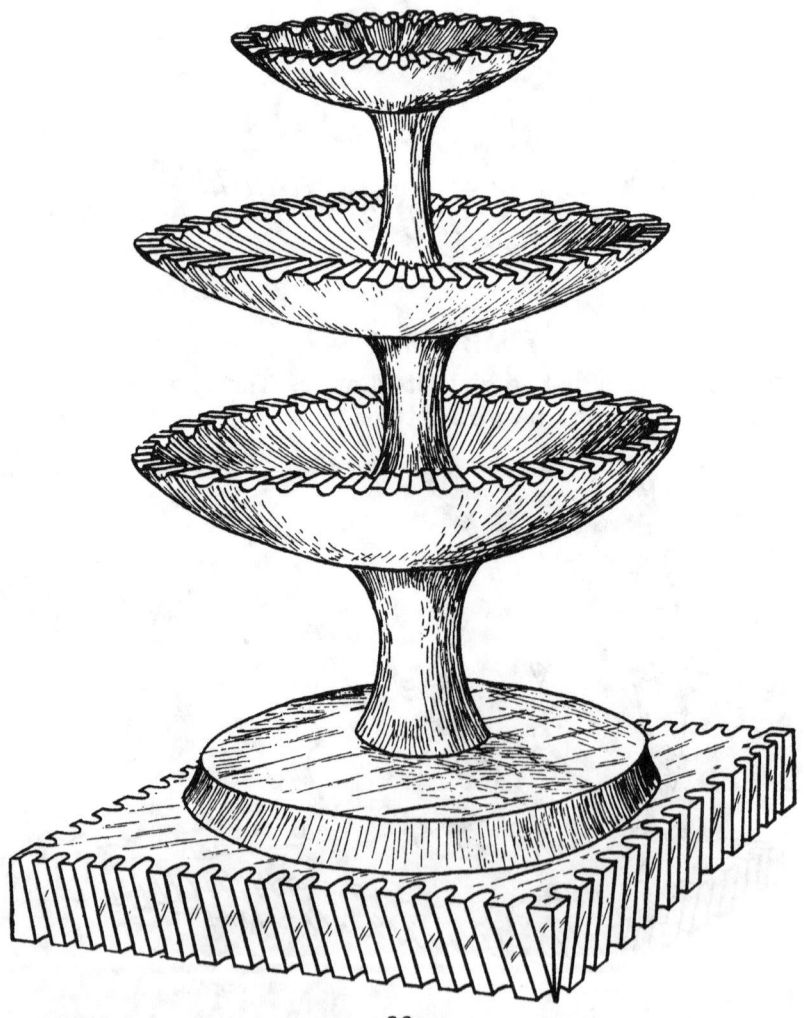

LIGHT HOUSE

This is a fine center piece. To make it high enough it is advise-able to freeze two pieces of ice together, one on top of the other. A piece of this type is usually hollowed out and illuminated with red and green lights. The windows may be burned in with a hot iron but care must be taken not to make them too large.

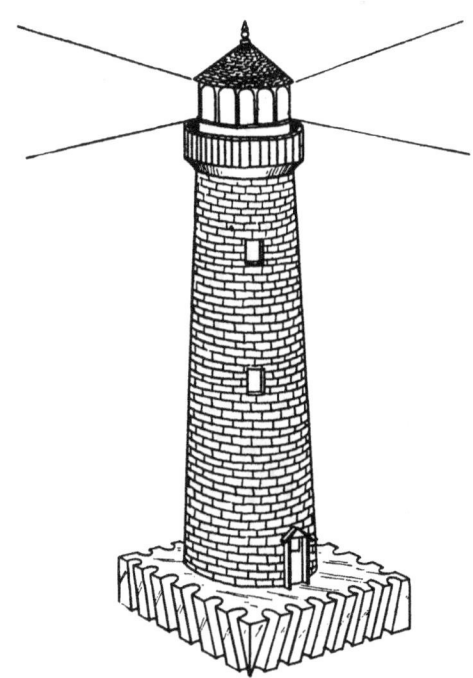

WHEELBARROW

This makes a suitable container for fresh flowers. Also it may be filled with fine chopped ice on which is placed a bowl of caviar, shrimps, or lobster salad.

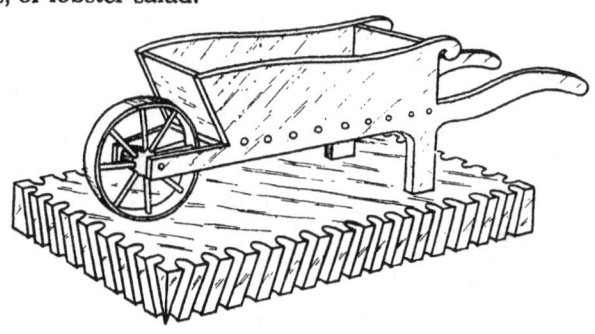

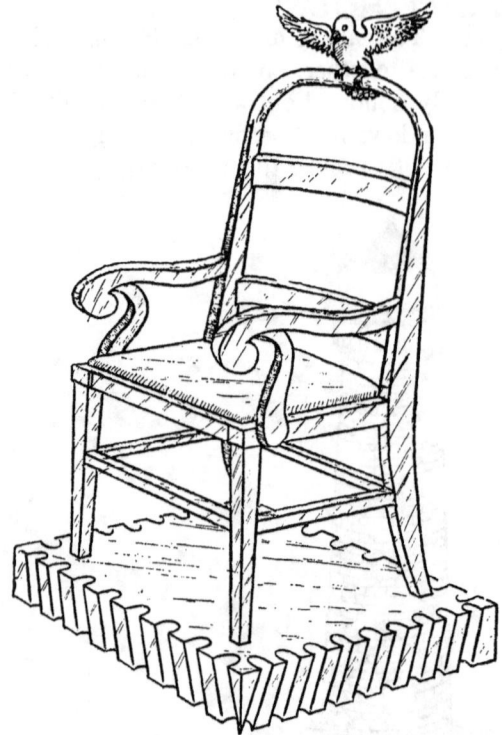

CHAIRS

Such pieces are made for furniture shows or furniture manufacturers' conventions. They may be made with or without the bird on top.

BEDS

Beds may be made in various designs. The cover may be made of shaved ice or colored water sprayed on.

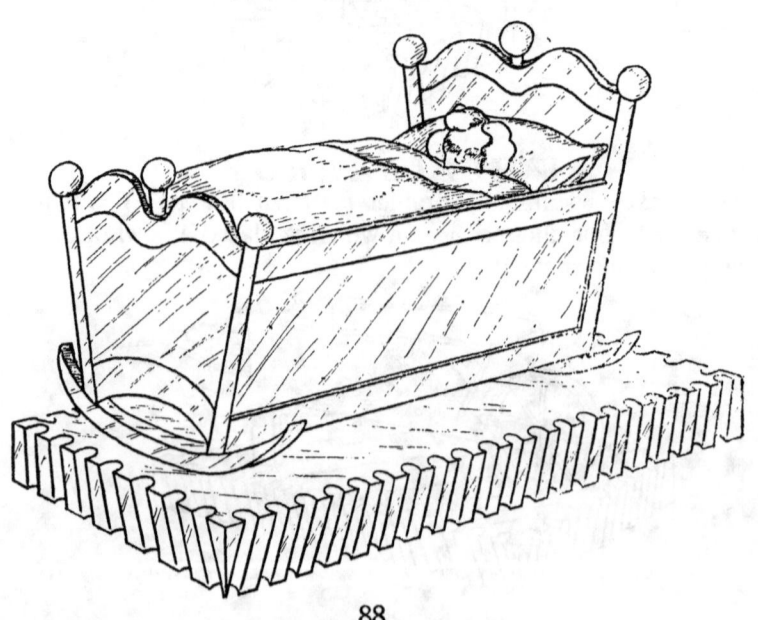

LOCOMOTIVES

This piece is effective if two batteries with colored lights are used, one below the smokestack and one in the boiler. Two more colored lights may be placed in the base. Line the coal car with napkins and place in here chunks of chocolate ice cream to represent coal. When serving the party turn out the lights. This is a very effective way of serving ice cream.

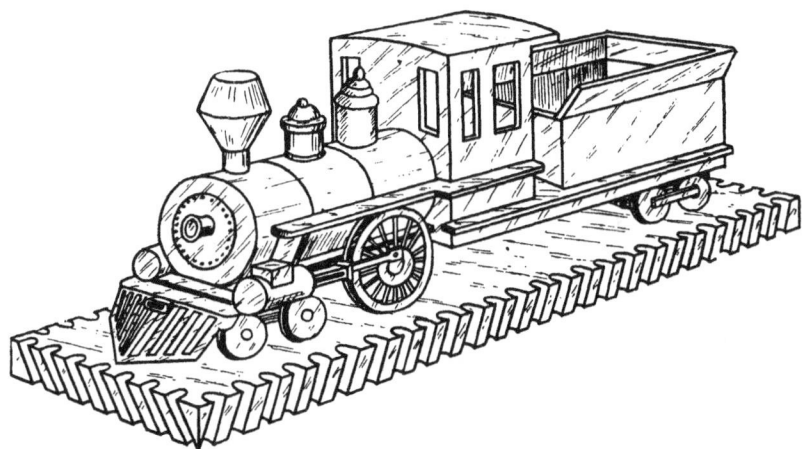

AUTOMOBILES

The rear seat of this piece may be used for fresh flowers or filled with shaved ice on which a bowl is placed filled with caviar or salad.

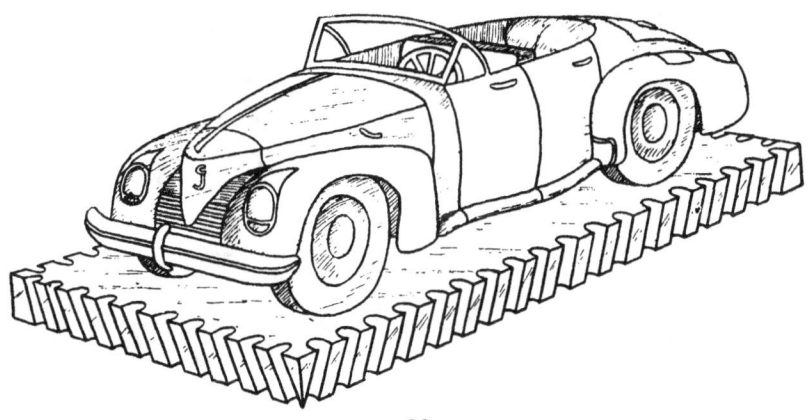

LAMPS

These all need batteries and bulbs. Some may be colored; some not. The one with double shade uses two pieces hollowed out and frozen together. The lamp post uses several blocks of ice.

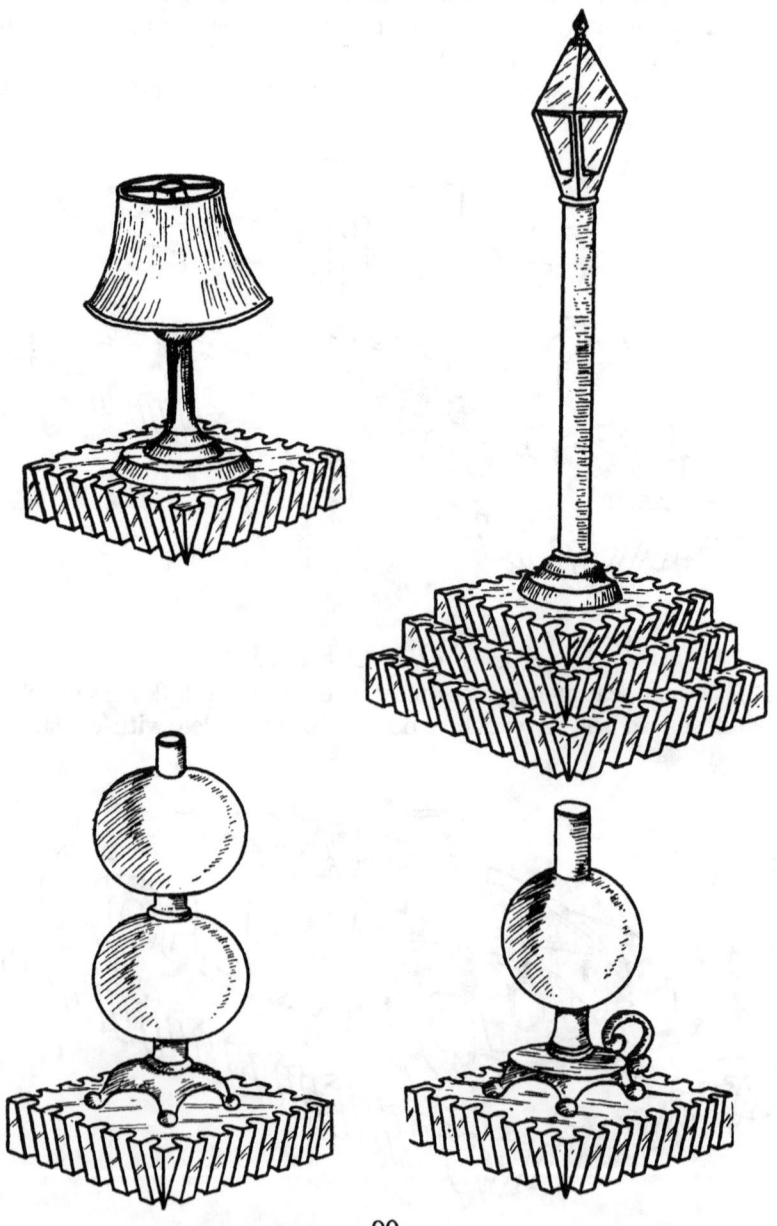

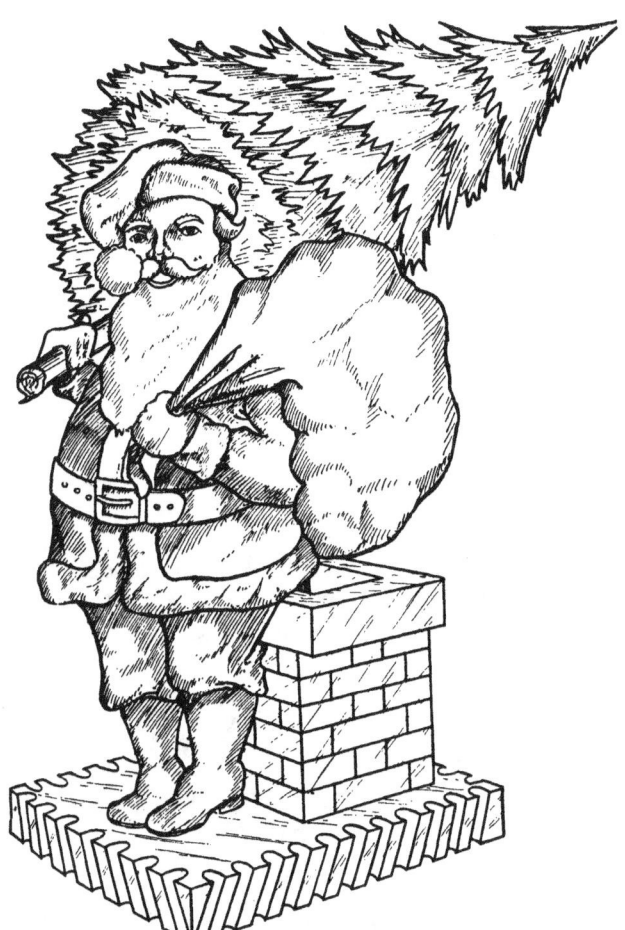

SANTA CLAUS

This may require two or more pieces of ice frozen together. The tree might be made separately and frozen to the rest of the piece. If this is done, make it of green colored ice. You might also spray water, colored red, on Santa's suit.

SLEDS

These are made in m a n y forms. On them may be placed baskets carved from ice and used for champagne buckets. They may also be used to hold bowls of salads.

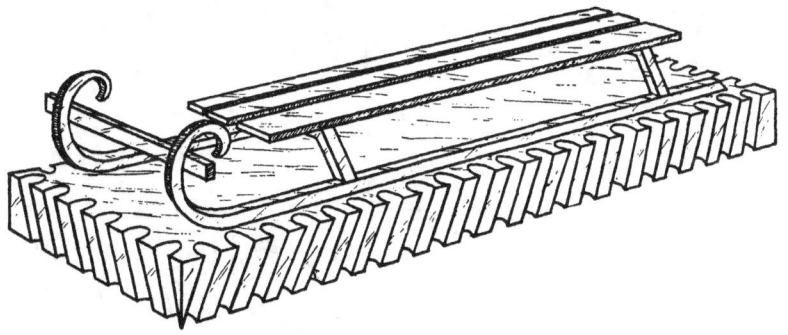

POTTERY

A number of subjects may be chosen for pottery. The important part is to get exact proportions. Hollow out the top, refill with shaved ice and insert a glass bowl for cold drinks.

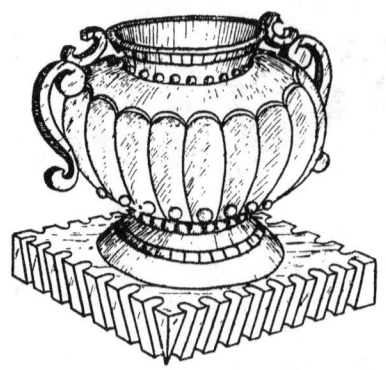

WISHING WELL

This requires a 400-pound piece of ice. The buckets are made separately and filled with caviar. The base may be covered with a white cloth and parsley placed on it to represent grass.

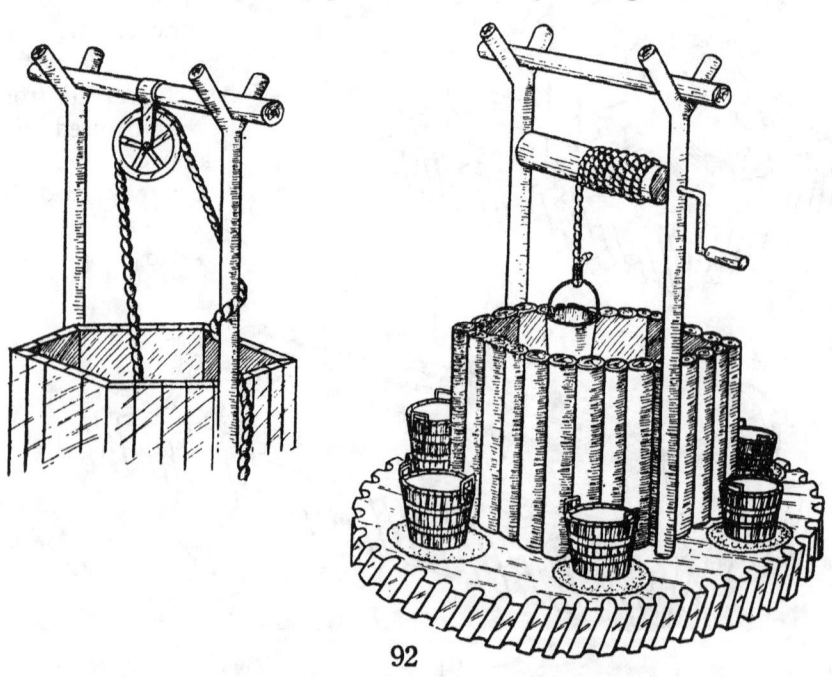

STEAMERS

Steamers are most effective if hollowed out and lighted. In burning in the port holes, be careful not to make them too large.

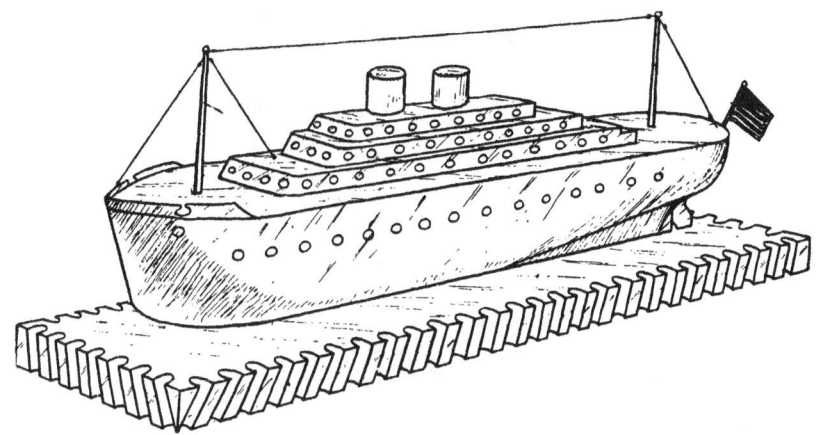

AIRPLANES

This design may also be hollowed out and lighted. The same precaution is true for the plane windows as for the ship's port holes.

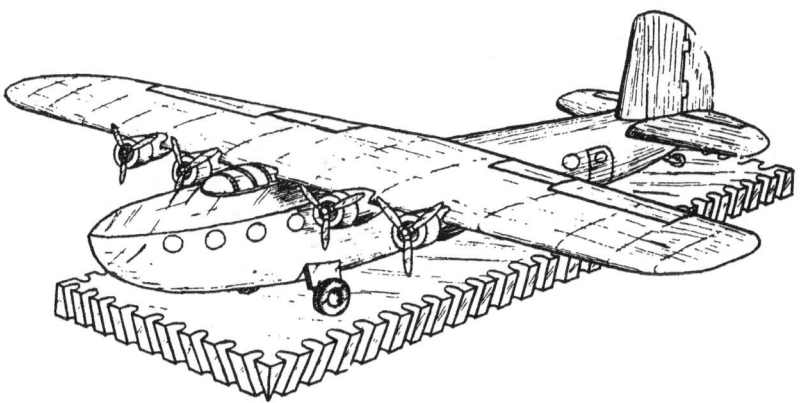

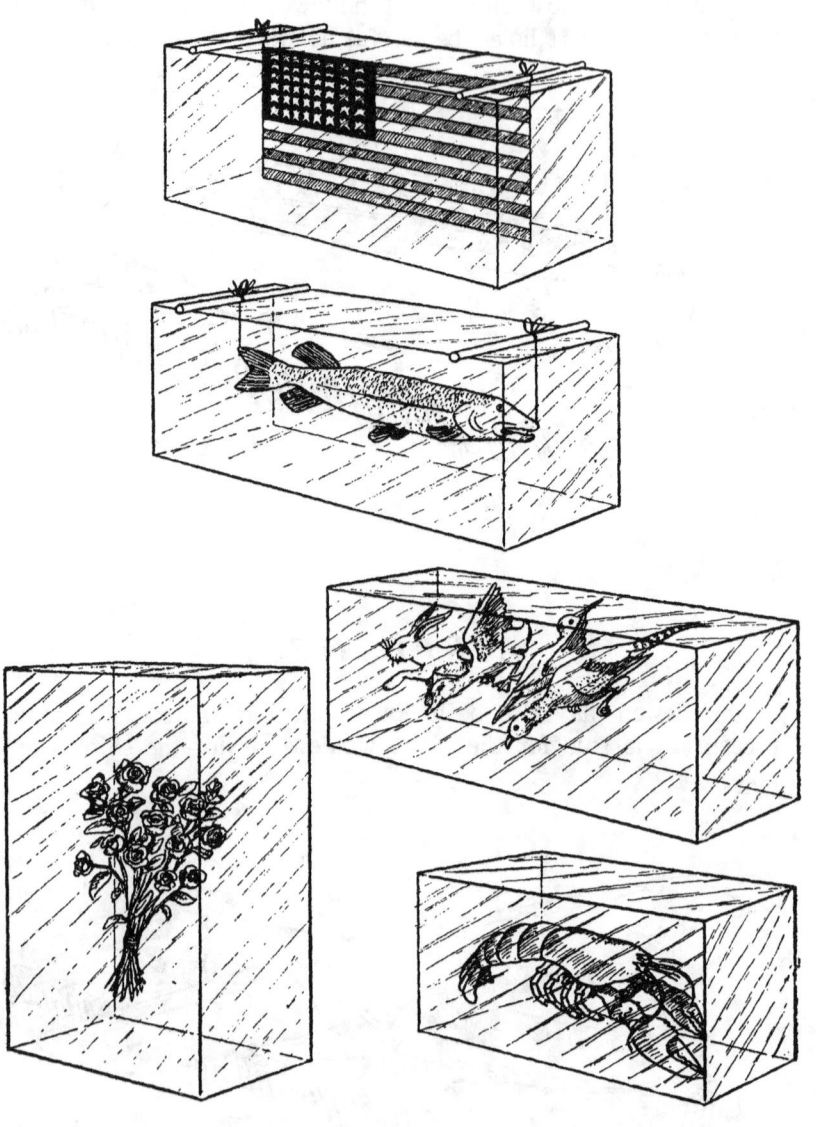

ARTICLES FROZEN IN ICE

Large fish, flags, flowers, and game may be frozen in ice blocks for food shows or for other kinds of display. To do this, saw part of the block off and hollow out the other part sufficiently to contain whatever object is to be frozen in the ice. Place the object in and fill the space with water. Cover this with the part which has been sawed away and allow the whole thing to stand overnight in freezing temperature. In the morning the desired piece is ready.

Another method is to place the object on a thin wire in a square, round, or rectangular mold. Fill the mold with water. When the water is partly frozen so that the object remains stationary, pull out the wire leaving the object in the middle of the block. Sometimes long objects such as a flag or a long fish are held in place by wires from the ends tied to sticks which are laid across the top of the mold. These may also be withdrawn when the ice is partly frozen. This method may be seen on the opposite page.

www.ingramcontent.com/pod-product-compliance
Lightning Source LLC
Chambersburg PA
CBHW072047190526
45165CB00019B/2136